# Blacks in
# America's Wars

# Blacks in America's Wars

## The Shift in Attitudes from the Revolutionary War to Vietnam

# Robert W. Mullen

**PATHFINDER**

New York    London    Montréal    Sydney

*To My Wife — Linda*

ISBN 0-913460-29-X paper; ISBN 0-913460-30-3 cloth
Library of Congress Catalog Card No. 73-89091
Manufactured in the United States of America

First edition, 1973
Eighth printing, March 1991

Published by the Anchor Foundation
**Distributed by Pathfinder**
410 West Street, New York, NY 10014, U.S.A.

Pathfinder distributors around the world:
Australia (and Asia and the Pacific):
  Pathfinder, 19 Terry St., Surry Hills, Sydney, NSW 2010
Britain (and Europe, Africa, and the Middle East):
  Pathfinder, 47 The Cut, London, SE1 8LL
Canada:
  Pathfinder, 6566, boul. St-Laurent, Montréal, Québec, H2S 3C6
Iceland:
  Pathfinder, Klapparstíg 26, 2d floor, 121 Reykjavík
New Zealand:
  Pathfinder, 157a Symonds Street, Auckland
Sweden:
  Pathfinder, Vikingagatan 10, S-113 42, Stockholm
United States (and Caribbean and Latin America):
  Pathfinder, 410 West Street, New York, NY 10014

Although the history of Black Americans is as old as American history, until very recently Blacks have been largely ignored in most treatments of American history. Except for generally cursory treatments of the lot of slaves, whether portrayed as happy or downtrodden, and except for a few paragraphs on the same few Black celebrities like Booker T. Washington and George Washington Carver, the Afro-American has been ignored.

With the rise of Black pride and the increased interest in Black history, the situation has improved somewhat. Afro-Americans are increasingly studying their own history, and rewriting American history to show the part played by their ancestors.

The United States is now coming out of one of the costliest and most brutal wars in its history, the war in Vietnam. There is no question that American involvement in Southeast Asia has been extremely unpopular in all sectors of the population. The opposition of young people, and particularly of students, has been discussed and analyzed by countless observers. But the opposition of Afro-Americans to the war has received little separate attention.

Black opposition to American policy in Southeast Asia deserves more attention than it has received for several reasons. It deserves this attention because the Afro-American population in its majority has opposed the war. But equally importantly, Black opposition to the war in Vietnam stands in marked contrast in several key ways to Black attitudes in previous wars. A comparison of these attitudes throws light on major changes in sentiments among Blacks about American society and how to change it.

Black Americans have taken part in all of this country's wars. Although white America usually restricted Black participation in military affairs until a crisis forced the utilization of Black troops, Black Americans have viewed their military record as proof of loyalty and as a claim to the benefits of full citizenship. [1]

Since United States law and tradition require citizens to participate in the armed forces, restriction of a group from fulfilling this obligation could provide a rationale for denying that group its full rights to citizenship. Aware of this reasoning, the Black American, therefore, sought to participate in America's wars in the hope that sacrifices on the battlefield would bring the reward of increased rights for all Black people in civilian life.

The life of Black people in America has been a strange paradox from the very beginning. A human being sold into slavery in Africa and brought to America as a slave, as moving and movable property, the Black man was subject to all the miseries that afflict any human, yet possessed no rights as a human being.

For much of American history Black people were frozen into one position. No matter what happened in the larger society, they remained slaves, unaffected by the political changes around them. When America won its independence from Great Britain, Blacks did not share in that independence. When the founding fathers declared that "all men are created equal" they did not mean the Afro-American.

With the winning of American independence and the establishment of the American form of government, the only recognition in the Constitution that Afro-Americans might bear some resemblance to human beings came as a result of the pressure of the slaveowners. The Southern slaveholders, anxious to increase their representation in the U. S. Congress, forced a provision into the Constitution counting each slave as three-fifths of a person for the purpose of representation, although naturally the slaves were not given their three-fifths of a vote.

Even after the abolition of slavery, Afro-Americans were in a peculiar position as citizens without full rights. Their unequal status naturally followed them into the armed forces. For three hundred years the Black soldier has found himself in an ambiguous position. In contrast to his white counterpart, the Black soldier could never be sure who his real enemy was or where his real battlefield was. Was his real battlefield at home or abroad? Was his real enemy next door or overseas?

Never completely accepted by his white comrades in arms or by his white neighbors at home, the Black soldier has repeatedly gone off to war in defense of a society which has excluded him from its benefits. More often than not, Afro-Americans saw participation in the armed forces as a way of fighting two battles simultaneously — while the real enemy was home-front racism and the real battlefield was in civilian society in the U. S., the Black soldier hoped to win the battle at home through his performance in the Army. Foremost in his mind has been the hope that recognition of his bravery would be rewarded by recognition as a full citizen at home. In every American war, on virtually every American battlefield, Black soldiers have paid a price in flesh and blood for a dream that remained denied.

The first American to shed blood in the revolution that freed America from British rule was Crispus Attucks, a Black seaman. Attucks, a slave and sailor, was killed by British troops in the Boston Massacre of March 5, 1770. Interestingly, this was an integrated massacre, with four white men joining Attucks as martyrs.

The martyrdom of Attucks pointed up the incongruity of the struggle against British colonialism. Attucks, as a seaman, probably felt the restrictions which Britain's new navigation acts imposed on colonial shipping. In this sense his interests in the struggle were similar to those of his white comrades. However, Attucks was also a fugitive slave. Winning independence from Great Britain would scarcely provide him with personal freedom since the condition of slavery would exist regardless of who won.

It was natural for many colonists to begin to question

*Above: Detail of an engraving of the Boston Massacre by Paul Revere which appeared in the* Boston Gazette *on March 12, 1770.*

*Below: Advertisement in the* Boston Gazette, *October 1750, offering a reward of ten pounds for the return of runaway slave Crispus Attucks, killed twenty years later in Boston.*

R AN-away from his Maſter *William Brown* of *Framingham*, on the 30th of *Sept.* laſt, a Molatto Fellow, about 27 Years of Age, named *Crispas*, 6 Feet twoInches high, ſhort curl'd Hair, his Knees nearer together than common; had on a light colour'd Bearſkin Coat, plain brown Fuſtian Jacket, or brown all-Wool one, new Buckſkin Breeches, blue YarnStockings, and a check'd woollenShirt.

Whoever ſhall take up ſaid Run-away, and convey him to his aboveſaidMaſter, ſhall have *ten Pounds*, old Tenor Reward, and all neceſſary Charges paid. And allMaſters of Veſſels and others, are hereby caution'd againſt concealing or carrying off ſaidServant onPenalty of the Law. *Boſton, October* 2. 1750.

the institution of slavery and link its abolition to the fight against England. Both the logic of demanding the right of independence for themselves, and the growth of Black demands for freedom, linked the two struggles in the minds of many colonists. At the same time that James Otis was writing his "Rights of the British Colonies," in which he affirmed that the Black slave also had an inalienable right to freedom, Blacks themselves were petitioning the General Court of Massachusetts for their freedom on the grounds that it was their natural right.

The Attucks incident in March 1770 impressed the more thoughtful of the colonists with the incongruity of their position. Its significance lay, as John Hope Franklin has observed, in the connection "which it pointed out between the struggle against England and the status of Negroes in America. Here·was a fugitive slave who . . . was willing to resist England to the point of giving his life. It was a remarkable thing, the colonists reasoned, to have their fight for freedom waged by one who was not as free as they."[2]

Although fear of slave revolts caused the colonists to exclude Blacks from militia service during much of the eighteenth century, Blacks served in the French and Indian Wars and early developed a tradition of military service that was still alive at the time of the Revolutionary War.

As early as the battles of Lexington and Concord in April 1775, Blacks took up arms against the mother country. Among the Black minutemen who participated in those famous battles were Peter Salem, Cato Stedman, Cuff Whittemore, Cato Wood, Prince Estabrook, Caesar Ferritt, Samuel Craft, Lemuel Haynes, and Pomp Blackman. One of the outstanding heroes of the Battle of Bunker Hill was Peter Salem, an ex-slave from Framingham, Massachusetts. Salem, according to some sources, fired the shot that killed Major John Pitcairn of the Royal Marines, the man second in command of the British expedition to Lexington.

Another Black man, Salem Poor, also distinguished himself at Bunker Hill. For his bravery during the battle, several officers commended Poor to the Continental Con-

11

*Peter Salem, in white shirt holding a rifle, at the battle of Bunker Hill.*

gress. Equally gallant at Bunker Hill were Pomp Fisk, Grant Coope, Charleston Eads, Seymour Burr, Titus Coburn, Cuff Hayes, and Caesar Dickenson. At least one Black soldier, Caesar Brown of Westford, Connecticut, was killed in action on Bunker Hill.

It must be pointed out that although Blacks distinguished themselves in the early battles of the Revolutionary War, they were by no means generally welcome in the revolutionary army in its early days. Shortly after General Washington took command of the Army, the white colonists decided that not only should no Black slaves or freemen be enlisted, but that those already serving in the Army should be dismissed.

On October 8, 1775, Washington and his staff discussed the question of using Black troops, and on November 12 an order was issued instructing recruiters "not to enlist Negroes, boys unable to bear arms, or old men unable to endure the fatigues of campaign."[3]

For General Washington, and for many other leaders

12

of the Continental Army, the question of using Blacks in the Army cut deep. Washington himself was a fourth generation slaveowner who owned or had on lease 160 slaves at the time of his death. The idea of recruiting and arming Blacks, whether slave or free, naturally raised fears of slave revolts.

Left to their own devices, the colonists would probably have kept the policy of excluding Blacks from military service throughout the war. But the situation was drastically changed for them by a proclamation by Lord Dunmore, the British governor of Virginia, in November 1775, which stated: "I do hereby . . . declare all . . . Negroes . . . free, that are able and willing to bear arms, they joining his Majesty's troops, as soon as may be, for the more speedily reducing this colony to a proper dignity."4

This proclamation raised the specter of a wholesale flight of slaves to the British colors, and caused the slaveowners considerable fear of slave mutinies and massacres as they imagined their former slaves, armed by the British, ravaging their plantations.

Therefore, the Americans could ill afford to alienate either slaves or freemen. The upshot was that Blacks were not expelled from the Army or refused enlistment, but on the contrary were accepted into the Continental Army with the proviso that they would receive their freedom at the end of their enlistment. Provisions were made, of course, for the government to pay compensation to the owners for all slaves freed in such way. The owners were to receive one thousand dollars while the freed slave would receive fifty dollars at the end of his enlistment.

Scarcely a month after Lord Dunmore's proclamation, General Washington's exclusionary policy was officially reversed and free Negroes were permitted to enlist. In addition, most states now began to enlist both slaves and free Negroes. Before the end of the war, most states, as well as the Continental Congress, had the policy of enlisting slaves with the previously mentioned proviso that they would receive their freedom at the end of their enlistment.

Of the 300,000 soldiers who served in the Continental Army during the War of Independence, approximately five thousand were Black. Some volunteered. Others were drafted. In addition to several all-Black companies, an all-Black regiment was recruited from Rhode Island. This regiment distinguished itself in the Battle of Rhode Island on August 29, 1778.

There was hardly a major battle between 1775 and 1781 that was without Black participants. Blacks were at Lexington, Concord, Ticonderoga, White Plains, Bennington, Brandywine, Saratoga, Savannah, and Yorktown. Two Blacks, Prince Whipple and Oliver Cromwell, crossed the Delaware with Washington on Christmas Day, 1776. Some won recognition and a place in the history of the War of Independence by their outstanding service, although most have remained anonymous.

Despite the contribution of Blacks to the winning of American independence, the new republic they helped form withheld freedom from the vast majority of its Black population. With the end of the war, many Blacks had lost their lives, and few had gained their freedom.

When war came again in 1812, Blacks once again had an opportunity to serve their country. Martin Delany, the great Black abolitionist and journalist, who was to serve as a major in the Civil War, described the temper and commitment of Blacks at the time. They were, he said, "as ready and as willing to volunteer in your service as any other." Blacks, he said, "were not compelled to go; they were not draughted [drafted]. They were volunteers."[5]

Afro-Americans fought against the British during the war on land and sea, and they were particularly conspicuous in the various naval battles fought on the Great Lakes under the command of Oliver H. Perry. It is estimated that at least one-tenth of the crews of the fleet in the lake region were Afro-American. Captain Perry originally objected to the assignment of Blacks to his ships. But after the Battle of Lake Erie, he was unstinting in their praise as men who "seemed insensible to danger."[6]

During these battles the legislature of New York also authorized the raising of two regiments of Black soldiers for its area, including slaves, with their masters' permission, and two battalions of Black soldiers were mobilized for the New Orleans area.

The mobilization for New Orleans was particularly significant because it was there on September 21, 1814, three months before the Battle of New Orleans, that General Andrew Jackson issued his proclamation "To the Free Colored Inhabitants of Louisiana." In that proclamation, Jackson, who needed to augment and strengthen his forces, called upon the free Blacks of Louisiana, which of course was a slave state, to answer the appeal of their country. In the appeal he confessed that "the policy of the United States in barring Negroes from the service had been a mistaken one."

The Jackson proclamation stated in part:

> As sons of Freedom you are now called upon to defend your most estimable blessings. As Americans, your country looks with confidence to her adopted children, for a valorous support, as a faithful return for the advantages enjoyed under her mild and equitable government. As fathers, husbands, and brothers, you are summoned to rally round the standard of the Eagle, to defend all which is dear in existence. . . . To every noble hearted free man of color, volunteering to serve during the present contest with Great Britain, and no longer, there will be paid the same bounty in money and lands now received by white soldiers. . . . The non-commissioned officers and privates will also be entitled to the same monthly pay and daily rations and clothes furnished to any American soldiers.[7]

On the eve of the Battle of New Orleans, December 18, 1814, Jackson, through his aide-de-camp Colonel Butler, issued another address to the Black soldiers who had, in Martin Delany's words, "proven themselves . . . worthy

15

*Black troops fought in Gen. Andrew Jackson's army against the British at New Orleans.*

of their country's trust, and in every way worthy of the proudest position of enfranchised freeman."[8] Jackson said to the Black troops:

> Soldiers! When on the banks of the Mobile, I called you to take up arms, inviting you to partake the perils and glory of your white fellow-citizens, I expected much from you; for I was not ignorant that you possessed qualities most formidable to an invading enemy. I knew with what fortitude you could endure hunger . . . the fatigues of a campaign. I knew well how you love your native country, and that you . . . had to defend what man holds most dear — his parents, wife, children, and property. You have done more than I expected. In addition to the previous qualities . . . I found among you noble enthusiasm . . . Soldiers! The President . . . shall hear how praiseworthy was your conduct in the hour of danger; and the representatives of the American people will give you the praise your exploits entitle you to.[9]

16

*Black sailor at Lake Champlain in the War of 1812.*

At the same time free Blacks were serving with Jackson's forces, other Blacks, runaway slaves, were crossing over to British lines. As during the Revolutionary War, the British offered freedom to all those slaves who joined them in fighting the Americans.

While it is not known how many slaves did fight with the British forces, groups of such ex-slaves were later found in Canada and the West Indies, to which they had been transported after the British withdrawal.

Some of those ex-slaves transported to the West Indies had been reenslaved by the British there. As with slaves who had been enrolled by their masters in the American army, many of the slaves fighting with the British found themselves again enslaved when the war was over and there was no further need for their military services.

The outbreak of the Civil War found the Black soldier in the "strangest paradox" of all.

In a war fought between Northern industrialists and Southern slaveowners to determine who would have hegemony over the federal government and who would be able to expand into the new territories of the West, the question of maintaining slavery where it already existed was not in contention when the war began.

Despite the fact that the war would eventually end the system of slavery, Black men were not even allowed to fight in the Union army when the war began. Because Lincoln was anxious to maintain the loyalty of the border states, in which slavery existed, he was adamant in refusing to consider using Black troops since their use "would support the view that it was an abolitionist war."[10]

For almost two years after the beginning of the war, the Lincoln administration continued to refuse to accept Black soldiers, contending the war was between white men and had nothing to do with Blacks, slave or free.

Among the arguments used to exclude Blacks from military service in the Civil War were some that were completely contradictory. On the one hand, it was argued that Blacks were unwilling to fight, especially against white Southerners. On the other hand, it was argued that if Blacks were given arms they might engage in a crusade to end slavery in the South and end up massacring the slaveowners. As Frederick Douglass, the Black abolitionist, explained to a Cooper Institute audience in New York in February 1863, whites claimed in one breath that Blacks would not fight and in the next that if they were armed they would become dangerous.[11]

Federal policy regarding slaves who ran away from their masters and came to the Union army was contradictory and confused in the first years of the war. Union officers often ordered fugitive slaves returned to their owners, and General Winfield Scott, writing in the name of President Lincoln in June 1861, even wrote Brigadier General McDowell asking him to allow owners of fugitive slaves in Virginia to cross the Potomac River in order

to recover slaves who had escaped to Union territory.
Despite the official coolness to runaway slaves, whenever the Union army appeared in an area there was an immediate flood of runaway slaves who made their way to Union lines. In fact, the magnitude of the movement was such that it is not quite fitting to call the process running away in the sense that the term was used before the outbreak of the war. Rather, it was a mass exodus. Often all the slaves in an area just picked up and went to the Union army, and in such numbers that they couldn't be returned.

The federal government and Union army only began to adopt a policy of allowing and even encouraging the recruitment of Blacks when it became clear that the war would be a long and drawn-out conflict in which it was essential to mobilize all the resources possible, and to weaken the enemy as much as possible.

In the early days of the war, in April 1861 when President Lincoln issued a call for 75,000 volunteers, Northern Blacks responded in great numbers, foreseeing that in the war against the Southern slaveholders, the abolition of slavery would eventually have to be used as a weapon against that class. Black companies and regiments were formed and ready to serve.

But neither Lincoln nor the governors of the Northern states had any intention of making use of Black troops. Negroes who presented themselves to recruiters were thanked for their troubles and sent home.

In July 1862 Congress authorized the use of Black troops in the Civil War. But there was no follow-up until January 1863 when the Emancipation Proclamation went into effect.

Both the decision to use Black soldiers in the Union army and the Emancipation Proclamation were the result of the desperate situation that the Northern forces found themselves in. Heavy losses plus increasing desertion by white troops were placing a premium on manpower. Dwindling white enlistments and the effective resistance by rebel units forced Lincoln to make an uncomfortable decision. Either he had to accede to the secession of the slave states,

*In 1862, Robert Smalls (above) was a young South Carolina slave serving on the Confederate gunboat, the* Planter. *The entire crew, except for the captain and two officers, was made up of Blacks. Smalls and the other crew members decided, in the Spring of 1862, to take over the ship and deliver it to the Union navy.*

*They waited for their chance. Finally, on the night of May 12, 1862, all three white officers went ashore. Smalls brought his wife and children, and the families of other crew members, aboard, and the crew made their preparations for the escape. They decided they had to pass through the heavy fortifications of Charleston's harbor as though on a routine run out to sea to reconnoiter. All agreed that if the plan failed and they were discovered, they would sink the ship and all would drown themselves, including the seven children aboard.*

*At 3 a.m. they fired up the boilers and cast off their lines. Passing the port batteries they gave the appropriate signals and were cleared for leaving the harbor. Once out of range of the Ft. Sumter batteries, they pulled down the Confederate flag, hoisted a bed-sheet, and made for the Union blockade fleet. Upon turning the vessel over to the Union navy, Smalls commented: "I thought the* Planter *might be of some use to Uncle Abe."*

or he had to transform the war into a war for the total destruction of the slave system, thereby unleashing and encouraging the pro-Northern sympathies of the millions of slaves in the Confederate States.

The Emancipation Proclamation of January 1, 1863, which freed all slaves in the rebel states and stipulated that freed slaves should be received into the armed forces of the United States, indicated that Lincoln had accepted the proposition that the North could only win the war by destroying the slave base of the Confederate States.

The Emancipation Proclamation was issued for another reason as well. The British ruling class had been virtually unanimous in its support for the Confederacy, seeing the war as a war between the Southern agricultural free-traders and the Northern industrial high-tariff forces. Free-trade Britain, wanting access for its industrial goods in the American market, naturally sided with the South against its Northern rival in this conflict and, in 1862, seemed about to recognize the Confederacy.

The Emancipation Proclamation, however, changed the situation considerably. With its promulgation, massive pro-Northern demonstrations and meetings took place among English workers, making it politically inexpedient for the British government to recognize the South.

Once the decision was made to permit the enlistment of Blacks in the army, Black abolitionists like Frederick Douglass and Martin Delany began to act as recruiting agents for the Union army in the North, holding rallies to enlist Afro-Americans. Douglass urged his fellow Blacks to "fly to arms, and smite with death the power that would bury the government and your liberty in the same hopeless grave." It was better to die free than to live as slaves, he said. [12]

He pointed out that he had "implored the imperiled nation to unchain against her foes her powerful Black hand. Slowly . . . that appeal is beginning to be heeded." [13]

In answering those who said that this was a white man's war, which had little to do with Black people, Douglass presented a long list of reasons Blacks should join the Army. Among these were the need to prevent the country "from drifting back into the whirlpool of pro-slavery compromise," the fact that Blacks should learn the use of arms in order to secure and defend their liberty, that battles would give Blacks a chance to demonstrate their courage, and that army service would help the Black man regain his self-respect. [14]

Douglass saw that the freed slaves would have a powerful argument in their future demands for full rights of citizenship if they played a conspicuous role in the army. In his words, "Once let the Black man get upon his person the brass letters, U. S.; let him get an eagle on his button . . . bullets in his pocket, and there is no power on earth . . . which can deny that he has earned the right to citizenship in the United States." [15]

Although there were some local decisions to recruit Southern Blacks into the Union army prior to the Emancipation Proclamation, these attempts were generally rebuffed by the War Department. In 1862, for example, General Hunter, who was trying to hold the whole coast of Georgia, South Carolina, and Florida with only 11,000 men, and whose frequent requests for reenforcements from the North went unfulfilled, decided to raise a Black regiment in the Spring of 1862. He had a great deal of success and spoke very highly of the conduct of his Black troops, and of their eagerness to get into battle. But the War Department later repealed his efforts.

After the Emancipation Proclamation, however, the War Department moved rapidly to begin enlisting Blacks. In January 1863 it authorized Massachusetts to raise two Black regiments, the first officially authorized Black units. Eventually nearly 200,000 Black troops were to serve in the Union army, and another 300,000 served as army laborers, spies, servants, and helpers. Lincoln admitted that their participation was essential to the victory in the war.

Eventually there were 154 Black regiments in the army, including 140 infantry units. They saw action in 198 battles and skirmishes and suffered 68,178 fatalities on the battlefield in the course of the war.

Of the nearly 200,000 Black troops to take part, 93,000

came from the slave states that had seceded, about 40,000 came from the border slave states, and the remainder from the North. By the end of the war there was scarcely a battle in which Black troops had not participated. Perhaps their outstanding achievement was the charge of the Third Brigade of the Eighteenth Division on the Confederate fortifications on New Market Heights near Richmond, Virginia. For their gallantry in that engagement Black soldiers received thirteen Congressional Medals of Honor in one day. In all, twenty Blacks received the medal in recognition of "gallantry and intrepidity" in combat during the Civil War. [16]

John Hope Franklin estimates that the Black mortality rate in the Army was nearly 40 percent higher than among white soldiers. This was partially due to unfavorable conditions, poor equipment, bad medical care, and the rapidity with which the Blacks were sent into battle. [17] But Black troops were also, as W.E.B. Du Bois pointed out, "repeatedly and deliberately used as shock troops, when there was little or no hope of success." [18]

The attitude of the Black soldiers in the Civil War can perhaps be best summed up in the words of a song which was widely popular among them during the conflict. This song, the marching song of the First Arkansas Colored Regiment of the Union army, was sung to the tune of "John Brown's Body."

Oh, we're the bully soldiers of the "First of Arkansas,"
We are fighting for the Union, we are fighting for the law,
We can hit a Rebel further than a white man ever saw,
    As we go marching on.

    *Chorus:*
    Glory, glory, hallelujah,
    Glory, glory, hallelujah,
    Glory, glory, hallelujah,
    As we go marching on.

See, there above the center, where the flag is waving bright,

We are going out of slavery, we're bound for freedom's
light;
We mean to show Jeff Davis how the Africans can fight,
As we go marching on!

We have done with hoeing cotton, we have done with
hoeing corn,
We are colored Yankee soldiers, now, as sure as you
are born;
When the masters hear us yelling, they'll think it's Gabriel's
horn,
As it went sounding on.

They will have to pay us wages, the wages of their sin,
They will have to bow their foreheads to their colored
kith and kin,
They will have to give us house-room, or the roof shall
tumble in!
As we go marching on.

They said, "Now colored brethren, you shall be forever
free,
From the first of January, eighteen hundred sixty-three."
We heard it in the river going rushing to the sea,
As it went sounding on.

Father Abraham has spoken and the message has been
sent,
The prison doors he opened, and out the prisoners went,
To join the sable army of the "African descent,"
As we go marching on.

Then fall in, colored brethren, you'd better do it soon,
Don't you hear the drum a-beating the Yankee Doodle
tune?
We are with you now this morning, we'll be far away
at noon,
As we go marching on.

Blacks also played a conspicuous role in the Union

24

*54th Massachusetts Colored Regiment, in which two of Frederick Douglass's sons served, attacks Ft. Wagner, S. C. For a year it refused to draw its pay, protesting against the fact that white privates earned $13 per month and Black privates only $7.*

*Above: Confederates massacring captured Black soldiers at Ft. Pillow in April 1864. All the captured Blacks, some 300 in all, were murdered. Five were buried alive.*

*Below: Black cavalrymen bringing in Confederate prisoners.*

Harriet Tubman, an escaped slave herself, led hundreds of others to freedom on the Underground Railway, despite a price of $40,000 on her head. In the Civil War she was a spy, scout, and nurse in the Union army in the South.

*Black infantry troops in front of barracks at Ft. Lincoln.*

*Civil War artillery battery.*

*Above: Confederates using bloodhounds attack the First South Carolina Colored Regiment at Pocatalago Bridge, 1862.*
*Left: Martin Delany, the abolitionist leader, was a major in the 104th Regiment. He was the first Black field officer in the Civil War.*

navy during the Civil War. Throughout its history the navy had not barred free Blacks from enlisting. In September 1861, suffering from an acute shortage of manpower, the navy went a step further and adopted a policy of signing up escaped slaves as well as free Blacks.

Because of the shortage of sailors, which continued throughout the war, the Navy treated Blacks fairly well since it was anxious to recruit them and have them re-enlist.

Black seamen comprised one-quarter of the sailors in the Union fleet. Of the 118,044 enlistments during the Civil War, 29,511 were Blacks. Some of the ships in the fleet were manned by predominantly Black crews, and there was scarcely a ship that didn't have some Afro-American crew members.

Because of the close quarters on warships, it was never practical to segregate the Blacks within the crews, the same way the army did in all-Black units, and for that reason the navy was not only integrated as a service, but also was integrated within each ship.

Martin Delany, appointed a major in the Union army late in the Civil War, explained why Blacks could justify their participation in the early wars of America: "Our common country is the United States. Here were we born . . . educated; here are the scenes of childhood . . . and from here will we not be driven by any policy that may be schemed against us."[19]

On the basis of being American and having a birthright citizenship, he said: ". . . natural claims upon the country . . . natural rights, which may, by virtue of unjust laws, be obstructed, never can be annulled. . . . It is this simple but great principle of primitive rights, that forms the fundamental basis of citizenship in all free countries, and it is upon this principle, that the rights of the colored man in this country to citizenship are fixed."[20]

For Delany, it was in the war record of Blacks that their claims to citizenship were justified. In serving one's country and fighting its battles there was no responsibility, notes Delany, "for which the country owes a greater debt of gratitude."[21] In Delany's words: "love of country, is the first requisition and highest attribute of every citizen; and he who voluntarily ventures his own safety for that of his country, is a patriot of the purest character."[22]

Blacks at the start of the twentieth century also attempted to justify their citizenship by recalling the war record of Blacks and in particular their role in the Civil War. Among those writers were Timothy Thomas Fortune and Rev. Hightower Kealing. Fortune was the editor of the *New York Age,* the influential weekly Black newspaper in the 1880s and 1890s. Kealing was a leading cleric in the African Methodist Episcopal Church of the times. In describing the general characteristics of Black people, Kealing also described the conduct of Blacks in the Civil War.

They were, he said, "affectionate and without vindictiveness." Slaves almost never did physical harm to their owners during the war, despite the fact that many of their masters were in the Confederate army and had left the slaves in the care of their wives and old and infirm white men. Their patience, he said, was the marvel of the world and had led many to question their courage until the battles of the Civil War demonstrated that Blacks were as courageous as whites.[23]

Kealing noted that the war record of the Black soldier was "without blot or blemish. His commanders . . . pronouncing him admirable for courage in the field . . . obedience in camp. That he should exhibit such excellent fighting qualities . . . and yet exercise the forbearance that characterizes him as a citizen, is remarkable."[24]

T. Thomas Fortune described the Black combat record in the Civil War in these terms: "However he may be lacking in pride of ancestry and race, no one can accuse the Negro of lack of pride of Nation. . . . Indeed, his pride in the Republic . . . [is] among the most pathetic phases of his pathetic history. . . . He has given everything to the Republic. . . . What has the Republic given him, but blows and rebuffs and criminal ingratitude!"[25]

With the Civil War over, Black soldiers found that they had achieved the legal status of freemen and the Four-

*In 1877 Henry O. Flipper, the son of former slaves, was the first Black graduate of West Point. During his four years there he was totally shunned by his classmates. After graduation, he was a second lieutenant in the all-Black Tenth Cavalry which was fighting Indians on the frontier. Dismissed from the army in 1882, due to a superior officer's racism, he stayed in the West, becoming a successful engineer.*

teenth and Fifteenth Amendments to the Constitution had given them the legal rights of citizenship. Once again, as in the Revolutionary War and the War of 1812, wartime manpower shortages had forced some kind of tolerance.

But with the war over, the need for Black support diminished and with no jobs, no money, and no training, Blacks found that they had exchanged legal slavery for economic slavery. When the government reneged on its promise of forty acres and a mule, Blacks found themselves without the economic resources to begin as small farmers and were forced into the status of agricultural laborers or sharecropers. Displaced and deserted by the very Union forces they had aided, Blacks found, as Addison Gayle points out, that their fight for liberty was in the final analysis no more than a fight for reenslavement, this time by the Black Code laws that swept the South after the abandonment of Reconstruction by the Federal government. [26]

*Charles Young was the third Black to attend West Point, graduating in 1889. He later was a major in the Spanish-American War and served in Cuba, the Philippines, Mexico, and Haiti. In 1916 Young was made a lieutenant-colonel.*

When the army was reorganized in 1866 and put on a peacetime basis, six Black regiments were established by law as a part of the regular army and as recognition and reward for valor. By an act of Congress in 1866, four regiments—the Twenty-fourth and Twenty-fifth Infantry and the Ninth and Tenth Cavalry—were organized as permanent army units and stationed west of the Mississippi River. Most of the officers in these units were white. The best-known graduate of these regiments was Gen. John Pershing, who earned the nickname "Black Jack" because of his service with Black soldiers.

The Ninth and Tenth Cavalry were later central units in the campaign to "win the West" between 1870 and 1900. These units became known as the "Buffalo Soldiers" and were widely feared by the Indians because of their toughness. Benjamin O. Davis, Sr., who was later to win fame as the first Black general during World War II, began his career with the Buffalo Soldiers.

When the Spanish-American War began, the total strength of the regular army was only 28,000 men. Among these were the four Black regiments that had been incorporated into the regular army after the Civil War and that had been very active in the Indian wars on the Western frontier. These regiments were to play a conspicuous role in American operations in both Cuba and the Philippines. During the course of the war six Blacks received the Congressional Medal of Honor.

Afro-American troops were involved in the war against Spain from the beginning. There were at least thirty Blacks on the battleship Maine when it blew up, of whom twenty-two were killed.

In the ensuing jingoist campaign for war with Spain, Blacks, too, shared the whipped up indignation and anger over the loss of life. In addition, the official propaganda about fighting a war to free our "little brown brothers," the Cubans, Puerto Ricans, and Filipinos suffering under the yoke of the despotic Spanish, struck a responsive chord among Afro-Americans.

Initial Black support for the Spanish-American War was also intensified by the fact that this was the first war since Blacks had gained their freedom in the Civil War, and it took place at a time when the racial oppression against them had been intensifying for several decades. For that reason, many Blacks saw participation in the war against Spain as an ideal chance to prove their right to citizenship and equality.

As a result, when the President called for 200,000 volunteers to supplement the inadequate regular army, Blacks were as enthusiastic about enlisting as any group in America. In addition to the four Black outfits in the regular army, numerous other Black groups served in the war against Spain. Several states, including Southern states, changed their initial ambivalence or hostility towards Black volunteers and permitted them to organize outfits and enter the service. Originally all these outfits were denied the right to have Black officers. But a widespread campaign around the slogan "No officers, no fight" succeeded in winning some concessions. In all, approximately one-hundred officers were commissioned in the volunteer units in the course of the war.

Among the Black outfits to participate in the conflict were the Third Alabama Infantry of Volunteers, the Third North Carolina Infantry, the Ninth Ohio Infantry, two companies of the Indiana Infantry, and Company L of the Sixth Massachusetts Infantry, the only Black company that was an integral part of a white regiment. But in the swift and decisive action that brought victory in the Caribbean, only those in the four regular Black outfits saw any considerable service.

The attitude of Black soldiers during the campaigns in Cuba can perhaps be best summed up in the words spoken by a Black colonel of the Eighth Illinois Regiment to his troops. "If we fail," he said, "the whole race will have to shoulder the burden."[27]

In fact, Black troops played a conspicuous part in all three of the major Cuban campaigns. Their performance was to be a source of pride to Afro-Americans for years afterwards.

In the fighting in Cuba, most of the Black regulars saw action and won the praise of their white officers. Many claim that the Black Ninth and Tenth Cavalry, which came to the aid of Theodore Roosevelt and his "Rough Riders," saved them from complete annihilation. Roosevelt himself was lavish in his praise of the Black soldiers at the time, and the exploits of these troops were heralded in newspapers across the country.

After the war ended, however, their exploits were relegated to the background as the aura around Roosevelt and the Rough Riders grew. Roosevelt himself, in his later remarks on Black troops in Cuba, was to change his original observations of their bravery, writing a year later that the Blacks were dependent on their white officers and that they frequently weakened and drifted to the rear of the battle.

When U.S. forces ended Spanish resistance in Cuba and Puerto Rico, they turned their attention towards the Philippine Islands. But in contrast to the campaigns in

*Detail of a painting by
Fletcher C. Ransom depicts
Troop C, Ninth United States
Cavalry, in the charge up
San Juan Hill in Cuba
during the Spanish-American
War. The Ninth Cavalry was
joined by Teddy Roosevelt's
"Rough Riders" in the attack.*

*When the Spanish-
American War
began, many
Blacks rushed to
join the army.
These recruits
are being drilled
in the manual
of arms at an
army camp in
Chattanooga in
1898.*

the Caribbean, there was widespread public opposition
in the United States to involvement in the Philippines.

The war in the Philippines was unpopular with the
American people for many reasons. Many Americans
felt that the acquisition of a colonial dependency was a
violation of the Declaration of Independence. Some were
opposed to the expenses of maintaining a colonial empire.
Others feared the competition of cheap Filipino labor
and agricultural goods.

In the Philippines, an independence movement led by
Emilio Aguinaldo had already been fighting the Spanish.
Between 1899 and 1902, 70,000 U.S. troops were sent
to the Philippines to put down his movement, which had
turned against the United States when the Americans
showed their opposition to Philippine independence.

For three years, the United States Army engaged in
a bloody war against the Filipino guerrillas, a war which
in many ways paralleled counterinsurgency methods later
employed in Vietnam. Among the 70,000 U.S. troops were
the four regular army Black units.

Within the Black population of the United States as
a whole, there was considerable opposition to intervention
in the Philippines. Most Black newspapers and leaders

publicly supported the idea of Filipino independence and felt that the United States was wrong to begin to develop a colonial empire of nonwhite subjects. They could not help but feel that this could only have a deleterious effect on the relations between whites and Blacks in the United States itself. Even such normally cautious Black figures as Booker T. Washington felt they had to speak out for Filipino independence.

The Black troops themselves were placed in an extremely pointed dilemma by the U.S. actions in the Philippines. Most displayed considerable identification with the nonwhite Filipinos, an identification that was heightened by the fact that white soldiers generally referred to both Black troops and Filipinos as "niggers." But most also felt that a good military showing by Black troops in the Philippines would enhance the cause of all Blacks in the United States and tried to reconcile these conflicting sentiments.

Opposition to the war by Blacks became so loud that by 1899 the War Department questioned whether it would be wise to send any Black troops at all to the islands. One War Department official doubted that such troops "if brought face to face with their colored Filipino cousins could be made to fire on them."[28]

The question was finally resolved in favor of sending Black troops, and all four regular army regiments saw action in the war. As the Americanization of the islands progressed, and the color bars against Blacks and Filipinos also progressed, Black troops increasingly felt that they were being used in an unjust war, that they were in part responsible for the racism against Filipinos that they could see spreading with American control.

Although most Black soldiers swallowed their misgivings, with the hope that their actions would reflect favorably on Blacks in America, this was not a universal reaction. The desertion rate among the Black troops was very high. According to Stephen Bonsal, desertions from Negro regiments was very different from white desertions. While whites generally deserted after quarrels with officers, or because of opposition to discipline or laziness, Blacks deserted "for the purpose of joining the insurgents."[29]

*The Tenth Cavalry poses for its picture in Cuba.*

The Filipino guerrillas actively encouraged Blacks to desert. They regularly addressed posters to "The Colored American Soldier" in which they described the lynching and discrimination against Blacks in the United States and encouraged the Black troops not to be the instrument of their white masters' ambitions to oppress another "people of color." Blacks who deserted to the Filipino side were welcomed with open arms and often given positions of major responsibility.

Of all the Black deserters, the most famous was David Fagan of the Twenty-fourth Infantry. Fagan accepted a commission with Aguinaldo's forces and for two years wreaked havoc on the Americans.

The bulk of Black soldiers did not resort to desertion, however, and overcame whatever misgivings they had in the hope that the evil of oppressing Filipinos would at least have a salutary effect on the treatment of their Afro-American brothers and sisters in the United States. Their misgivings were, however, strong, as can be seen in the collection of letters from Black troops to Black newspapers which were gathered and reprinted by Willard B. Gatewood, Jr. in *Smoked Yankees.*

For the young Black man entering any branch of the armed forces today, it is hard to realize that the military was one of America's "most segregated institutions" at the start of the twentieth century.[30] Today, formal color barriers are absent throughout most of the military establishment. Equal treatment regardless of race is "official policy" in such non-duty facilities as chapels, post exchanges, movie theaters, dependents' housing, as well as military assignments, promotions, and living conditions. In fact, ironically, the armed forces are today far more integrated than the society they are supposed to defend.

However, in the early twentieth century, owing to a general rise in American racial tensions and outbreaks of violence between Black and white troops, opinion ran heavily against the use of Black soldiers. They were totally barred from the marines and were permitted to serve in the navy only in the most menial positions. Only the army permitted Blacks to serve in every branch except the elite pilot section of the Aviation Corps.

Two cases of mass punishment of Black soldiers, in Brownsville in 1906 and in Houston in 1917, illustrate the climate in which the Black troops had to function.

On the evening of August 13, 1906, a volley of shots rang out in Brownsville, Texas, where a great deal of tension existed between the townspeople and the all-Black Twenty-fifth Infantry stationed at nearby Fort Brown.

The soldiers thought they were being fired on to avenge the alleged attempted rape of a white woman by someone she described as Black. The townspeople themselves thought that they were being attacked by the troopers in response to previous racial slurs against them. When the shooting died down, one white man had been killed, a policeman was seriously injured, and 170 Black soldiers were charged with murder.

Townspeople accused the troops of three companies of the First Battalion, Twenty-fifth Infantry of the shooting, despite the fact that the white officers of those companies proved that the accused, to a man, had been asleep in their quarters when the shooting broke out.

The soldiers, for their part, denied any knowledge of the gunfight and signed statements proclaiming their innocence. In a situation where whites were accusing Blacks, the War Department was quick to come down on the side of the white townspeople. After an inconclusive investigation, President Theodore Roosevelt demanded that the guilty party step forward. When no soldier admitted to any guilt, Roosevelt signed an executive order drumming 170 Black troopers out of the Army with dishonorable discharges. This was done without a trial and without a shred of evidence against them. Many of the victimized Black troopers had fought at Roosevelt's side in Cuba.

Only sixty-six years later, in 1973, when only one of the original Black soldiers was still alive, did the government make amends for the injustice perpetrated on the Twenty-fifth Infantry by changing the discharges from dishonorable to honorable.

Southerners in Congress took advantage of the Brownsville incident to attack the record of Black troops in general. The feelings developed among large sections of the Black population that Roosevelt and the South had set out to discredit the claim of Afro-Americans to full citizenship by denigrating the fighting ability of Negro soldiers.

A second case of mass punishment of Black soldiers took place in November 1917 in Houston, Texas. Here sixty-four soldiers of the all-Black Twenty-fourth Infantry were accused of killing seventeen whites after pitched street battles, and were brought to trial under mob-rule circumstances.

In a one-day trial, the largest murder trial in American history, an all-white military tribunal sentenced thirteen of the convicted soldiers to death by hanging and the remaining forty-one to life imprisonment.

The trial sent shock waves through the Black communities in the United States and badly shook the pride of Blacks and their faith in the possibilities of fair treatment at the hands of white Americans.

Both the Brownsville and Houston incidents were significant because in both cases the army resorted to whole-

*Sixty-four members of the Twenty-fourth Infantry at their court-martial for mutiny and murder, November 1, 1917. All the members of the military tribunal, held at Ft. Sam Houston, Texas, were white.*

sale victimizations because the troops involved were Afro-Americans. Both incidents took place against a backdrop in which Black soldiers faced hostile and agressive white mobs whenever they left their posts and tried to assert their basic rights as human beings and American citizens.

Thus, despite the honors won in the Spanish-American War, the status of the Black American and the Black soldier plummeted to a new low in the early decades of the twentieth century. With the tightening of racial lines, "Black doughboys" had to once again fight for the right to die on an equal basis with whites in World War I.

For Black enlisted men and officers, World War I was deeply disturbing. Racial discrimination at home and abroad had reached staggering new heights and the government seemed to be going out of its way to emphasize the subordinate status of Black soldiers, most of whom were restricted to labor and service brigades.

The extent to which the government was willing to humiliate and degrade Black troops in order to placate the prevailing prejudice and racism among whites can be seen in an official order from General Pershing's office on August 7, 1918. The American Army realized that its foreign allies might not be aware of how Blacks were supposed to be treated and might end up making the terrible mistake of treating Blacks like human beings, which would have a bad effect on future race relations in the U. S. Army and in American society as a whole. To make sure that such mistakes did not occur, Pershing's office issued a memorandum entitled "To the French Military Mission — Secret Information Concerning Black American Troops." This memorandum stated in part:

1) prevent the rise of any "pronounced" degree of intimacy between French officers and Black officers.
2) do not eat with Blacks, shake hands, or seek to meet with them outside of military service.
3) do not commend "too highly" Black troops in the presence of white Americans.[31]

Despite this sort of virulent racism, Blacks did become actively involved in World War I. The Black American was affected by the rhetoric about "making the world safe for democracy" just as the white American was, despite the fact that most of America was not yet safe for democracy. Black leaders also raised the previously heard argument that "the race is on trial." A faculty and student club at Howard University, for instance, commented that "if we fail, our enemies will dub us COWARDS for all time; and we can never win our rightful place. But if we succeed — then eternal success."[32]

Shortly after the United States entered the war, Black leaders from different organizations adopted resolutions to express the attitudes and aspirations they thought were fitting for Black Americans in wartime. One of the arguments for Black support of the war was that despite the poor records of the United States, Britain, and other allies in dealing with colored people, "we earnestly believe that the greatest hope for ultimate democracy . . . lies on the side of the allies." They argued that Blacks should join in the "fight for world liberty" despite the insults and discrimination they suffer even while doing "their patriotic duty."[33]

Many Blacks hoped that participating in a fight for democracy around the world, as the war was being bally-hooed, would lead to their participation, too, in a bit of that democracy. Prominent whites lent support to this optimistic view of the war's impact on race relations. Theodore Roosevelt told Black audiences that America's war aim of securing greater international justice would lead to a "juster and fairer treatment in this country of colored people."[34] While there was considerable skepticism among the Black rank-and-file, most Black leaders called for complete devotion to the war effort and for the stifling and muffling of grievances until the war was over.

Even such Black leaders as W. E. B. Du Bois, who would later become much more cynical about the professed aims and desires of the United States government, counseled subordination of the Black struggle for human rights to the war effort. In an editorial entitled "Close Ranks!" in *Crisis* magazine in July 1918, Du Bois stated: "Let us not hesitate. Let us, while the war lasts, forget our special grievances and close ranks shoulder to shoulder with our white fellow citizens . . . fighting for democracy. We make no ordinary sacrifice, but we make it gladly and willingly with our eyes lifted to the hills."

The first duty of Afro-Americans, Du Bois stated, was to "close ranks" and fight with their white brothers rather than bargain with their loyalty and profiteer in the blood of their country.

Many other Blacks did not, however, appreciate Du Bois's advice. The Washington, D. C., branch of the National Association for the Advancement of Colored People felt the editorial was inconsistent with the work and spirit of the association. This group saw no reason to "stultify consciences" or act indifferent to the acts of injustice and indignity continually heaped on Blacks.

Other segments of the Black press attacked Du Bois for "selling out." But through it all Du Bois maintained that the proper attitude for the Black American was "first your country, then your rights."

Other Black leaders attacked the racial policies of President Woodrow Wilson himself. They argued that Wilson would never "make the world safe for democracy" when he had not been able to make America safe for it. They charged that during his administration, Wilson had transformed the nation's capital into the most segregated city outside the deep South. Government facilities, they pointed out, had been resegregated. "Colored" restrooms were established in government office buildings. The lynching rate nationally climbed as high as two Blacks a month. They further pointed out that Wilson himself had repeatedly declared this a "white man's war."

Despite this, Wilson put up little resistance to accepting Black troops. In fact, Wilson was reminded by the editor of one newspaper that the use of Black men was "a good thing." As the editor put it: "It seems a pity to waste good white men in battle with such a foe. The cost of sacrifice would be nearly equalized were the job assigned to Negro troops."[35]

Still the Afro-American heeded the call to arms to defend democracy and to win the war to "end all wars." He served in segregated units, generally under the command of white Southern officers. One of these officers welcomed his troops with the admonition: "You need not expect democratic treatment. . . . Don't go where your presence is not desired."[36] In short, feel free to die equally with white soldiers, but don't try to live equally.

Of the 750,000 men in the regular army and National Guard at the beginning of the war, about 20,000 were Black. The passage of the Selective Service Act on May 8, 1917, however, provided for the enlistment of "all able-bodied Americans between the ages of 21 and 31." On registration day, July 5, 1917, more than 700,000 Blacks registered for the draft. Before the end of the Selective Service enlistments, 2,290,525 Blacks had registered, of whom 370,000 were called into service.

Nearly 31 percent of the Afro-Americans who registered were drafted, while only 26 percent of the whites were taken. This was not due to the superior physical or mental qualifications of the Black registrants, but rather to

*The 369th Infantry, "Harlem Hell-Fighters," attached to the French army, were the first Allied troops to reach the Rhine in World War I.*

discrimination against them by draft boards on the question of deferments. One board in Georgia was discharged because of the crassness of its discrimination against Blacks seeking exemptions from service.

The first Black stevedore battalion arrived in France in June 1917. From then until the end of the war Blacks came in large numbers. Before the end of the war, more than 50,000 Blacks in 115 units comprised more than one-third of the entire American forces in Europe.

The German Army tried to use the discrimination against Blacks in the United States for propaganda advantage with Black doughboys. When it became clear to the Germans that the Ninety-second Division consisted almost entirely of Black soldiers, the Germans began circulating a leaflet pointing out the contradiction of fighting "for democracy" abroad without rights at home, and attempted to persuade the Black soldiers to lay down their arms. The leaflet said, in part, that Blacks should not be deluded into thinking that they were fighting for humanity and democracy. It asked whether Blacks had the same rights as white people or were second-class citizens. It asked if they could dine in the same restaurants as whites. It asked whether lynching was "a lawful proceeding in a democratic country."

After pointing out the answers to these questions, the leaflet then asked: "Why, then, fight the Germans only for the benefit of the Wall Street robbers and to protect the millions they have loaned to the British, French, and Italians?"

Despite the obvious truth of the German statements, the appeal had little direct effect.

The most successful Black units during the First World War were those attached to the French command. Of these four regiments, the 369th, 370th, 371st, and 372nd, three were awarded the *Croix de Guerre* by France. There were also numerous individual citations for acts of bravery. But in the U. S. Army, because of the racist assumptions about Black soldiers, the favorable aspects of the performance of the Afro-American troops was overlooked.

The Black American had hoped that in making the

*Well-wisher greets a "Harlem Hell-Fighter" during a victory parade. In all, the 369th suffered 1100 casualties in World War I.*

"world safe for democracy," America would grant more democracy to its largest minority. This optimism had been one of the factors behind the loyalty pledged by many Black leaders during the war. But, just as the "war to make the world safe for democracy" resulted for the world as a whole in nothing more than a redivision of the colonial world in favor of the victors so, too, in the United States itself the aftermath of the war saw Black hopes for full civil and human rights again dashed.

While the war was still going on, and one-third of the American troops were Black, ninety-six Blacks were lynched in 1917 and 1918. The Ku Klux Klan, revived in 1915, began its growth into a national organization in the early 1920s.

However, Black soldiers returning to the United States were now unwilling to allow the racists to attack them without fighting back. They returned with a determination to fight for their freedom at home, as they had been told they had just done abroad.

One editorial in the May 1919 issue of *Crisis* undertook to speak for the returning Black soldier with the following words: "We return from the slavery of uniform which the world's madness demanded us to don to the freedom of civilian garb. We stand again to look America squarely in the face and call a spade a spade. We sing: This country of ours . . . is yet a shameful land. It lynches . . . steals . . . insults us. . . . We return from fighting. We return fighting. Make way for Democracy. We saved it in France, and by the Great Jehovah, we will save it in the U. S. A., or know the reason why."[37]

One of the outstanding Black poets of the postwar period, Claude McKay, expressed the feelings of a great many returning Blacks when he wrote:

> If we must die, let it not be like hogs
> Hunted and penned in an inglorious spot,
> While round us bark the mad and hungry dogs,
> Making their mock at our accursed lot.
> If we must die, O let us nobly die,
> So that our precious blood may not be shed
> In vain; then even the monsters we defy
> Shall be constrained to honor us though dead!
> O kinsmen! we must meet the common foe!
> Though far outnumbered let us show us brave,
> And for their thousand blows deal one deathblow!
> What though before us lies the open grave?
> Like men we'll face the murderous, cowardly pack,
> Pressed to the wall, dying, but fighting back! [38]

More than seventy Black Americans were lynched during the first year following the war, some of them returned soldiers still in uniform. From June 1919 to the end of the year, approximately twenty-five race riots occurred in urban areas. The new element now was that Blacks were no longer the helpless victims, but rather fought back, killing some of the white attackers. Du Bois's theme of all Americans "closing ranks" was broken. He was to write in 1919: "By the God of Heaven, we are cowards and jackasses if now that the war is over, we do not marshal every ounce . . . to fight a . . . more unbending battle against the forces of hell in our land." [39]

Thus, despite the French honor that recognized Blacks as having "saved the most sacred cause, the liberty of the world," America was still not ready to "repay its debt." The returning veteran, after marching up Fifth Avenue in the Victory Parade, faced the rise of the Klan, one of America's "hottest" summers, and race riots across the country. After returning from the battle against Germany, the Black soldier had to face the battle against America.

Racial stereotypes and a continuing belief in the inferiority of the Afro-American were widespread among many Americans and among high-ranking officers of the military in the 1920s and 1930s. In the interwar period the army not only remained segregated, but it also adopted a policy of having a quota on Black enlistment in order to keep the number of Blacks proportional to the percentage of Afro-Americans in the United States as a whole. However, in the pre-World War II period the number of Blacks in the service never did approach this quota. On the eve of Pearl Harbor, Blacks constituted less than 6 percent of the Army. There were only five Black officers in the Army, three of whom were chaplains.

But during World War II Blacks again entered the service in large number, although at no time did they exceed 10 percent of the total personnel. They were again placed in segregated units, and approximately three-quarters served in the quartermaster and transportation corps.

The invasion of Ethiopia by Italy in 1935 had focused the attention of Afro-Americans on world affairs. Even the most provincial Blacks became concerned with international politics. Ethiopia was the only country in Africa which had retained its independence, and its defeat by Italy would symbolize the final victory of whites over Blacks. Therefore in many communities Blacks began to raise money and join support organizations for the defense of the Ethiopians against Italy.

Blacks also could not help but notice that Hitler's racist ideology was directed as much against them as against Jews. Along with the rest of America they watched how Hitler snubbed Black Olympic champions like Jesse Owens at the 1936 Berlin Olympics. Obviously Blacks could have no sympathy with either Mussolini's Italy or Hitler's Germany.

In spite of this, however, Blacks entered the Second World War with mixed emotions. They were going to defend the United States, a country just as influenced by racist ideology as Germany, a country where lynchings had become so commonplace and so much an ac-

51

cepted part of American life that an anti-lynching bill could not be passed in Congress, a country where the rate of lynchings during the years of the Roosevelt administration had risen to one per week.

Under the Selective Service Act of 1940, more than three million Afro-Americans registered for the draft. In 1942 about 370,000 Blacks entered the armed forces. In 1944, when the army was at its peak strength, there were about 700,000 Blacks in the army alone, and around 165,000 in the Navy, 5,000 in the Coast Guard, and 17,000 in the Marine Corps, which had begun admitting Blacks in 1942. There were no Black marine officers, however, during World War II. In the course of the entire war, approximately one million Afro-Americans served in the armed forces, which approximated their ratio in the population as a whole. All served in segregated units until the severe manpower shortages of 1945 forced the government to begin putting individual Blacks into previously all-white units as replacements.

Despite continuing official hostility and indifference, many Black units received the Presidential Citation for gallantry. There was no dearth of individual bravery either. Private Robert H. Brooks was the first member of the United States armored forces, and probably of the whole army, to give his life in the war against Japan, and Dorie Miller, a Navy mess attendant, was the first hero of the war. During the Pearl Harbor attack, Miller manned a machine gun and shot down four enemy planes. Later, he was awarded the Navy Cross.

On the home front, Blacks also gave support to the war effort. They purchased bonds and served in the Red Cross. However, in contrast to their state of mind at the outbreak of the First World War, Blacks had few illusions about the benefits their participation in the war would bring them. Any doubts they might have had were dispelled by the tremendous difficulties in securing work in the burgeoning defense industries.

The beginning of large-scale war production in the United States on the eve of World War II differed in one major respect from the situation in World War I. There were around three million unemployed whites when war production began to tool up for World War II, and most employers gave them first crack at new jobs opening up. The jobs that became available to Blacks were those that whites had abandoned in favor of the higher paying defense plant jobs.

The situation was graphically illustrated on the cover of the July 1940 *Crisis,* the magazine of the NAACP, which depicted air force planes flying over an aircraft factory turning out new planes. The caption across the picture read "For Whites Only." At the bottom of the cover was printed: "Negro Americans may not help build them, repair them or fly them, but they must help pay for them."

In January 1941, A. Philip Randolph, head of the Brotherhood of Sleeping Car Porters, announced plans for a March on Washington on July 1, 1941, to protest discrimination in war industry employment and segregation in the armed forces. He predicted that between 50,000 and 100,000 Blacks would participate in the demonstration.

The call for a March on Washington was received with great enthusiasm by Blacks all over the country, and thousands began to work on the campaign and make preparations to demonstrate. It also caused great consternation in government circles. Government officials kept asking "What will Berlin say?" — to which Blacks could reply that they were more interested about what Berlin would say about America's racist policies.

As the date for the March on Washington approached, the government put great pressure on Randolph to call off the demonstration. Eleanor Roosevelt and Fiorello La Guardia were sent to meet with him and try to coax him into canceling it. President Franklin D. Roosevelt called him to Washington to meet with him in hopes of securing his agreement to drop the plan.

In the discussions Roosevelt refused to consider desegregating the armed forces but agreed to issue an executive order forbidding discrimination in war industries.

One week before the march was scheduled to take place, Roosevelt signed Executive Order 8802, the Fair Employment Practices order, and Randolph, despite objections from some in his movement who wanted to hold out for desegregation of the armed forces as well, agreed to call off the march.

Randolph's attitude was indicative of a great difference in Black attitudes towards World War I and World War II. Whereas W. E. B. Du Bois's "Close Ranks!" editorial had reflected the view of most Black leaders in World War I—that Blacks must drop their own demands for the duration of the war and put country ahead of self—in World War II Blacks were in the main unwilling to defer their demands until the end of the war.

Faced with rampant discrimination in employment, segregation in the armed forces, and demeaning personal discrimination, Blacks reacted to the war not simply as Americans, but as Black Americans. When they were often turned away while trying to contribute blood to the Red Cross Blood program, when America, "the last bulwark of democracy," was planning separate air-raid shelters for Blacks and whites in Washington, D. C., when lynchings continued unabated during the war, when race riots broke out against Black GIs trying to use the same facilities as their white counterparts, it was only natural that Blacks should feel that they were involved in two simultaneous wars—one against Hitler in Germany, and the other against the Hitlers in the United States.

This attitude was embodied in the "Double V" concept among Blacks during the war—that the war must end in two victories, one against Hitler, one against American racism.

Many Afro-Americans took advantage of the war to tie their racial demands to the ideology for which the war was supposedly being fought. The Black press frequently compared the similarity of American treatment of Blacks and the Nazis' treatment of minorities, the white-supremacist doctrine in America and the master-race doctrine in Germany. Stimulated by the "democratic ideology of the war," Blacks increasingly were moved to reexamine their position in society. They found it simply too difficult to reconcile their treatment with the announced war aims.

As one observer put it: "The hypocrisy and paradox involved in fighting a world war for the four freedoms and against aggression by an enemy preaching a master race ideology, while at the same time upholding racial segregation . . . could not be overlooked. The war crisis provided American Negroes a unique opportunity to point out, for all to see, the difference between the American creed and practice. . . ."[40]

The refusal of the government and armed forces to end official segregation was one of the conditions that most disturbed Blacks during the war. On October 9, 1940, the White House issued a policy statement which refused to abandon the principle of segregation in the armed forces.

As the war progressed, the emotional impact of this issue grew. The hypocrisy involved in setting up a segregated army to fight an enemy with a master-race ideology was apparent to all Black troops. One result was that Blacks, on the average, "tended to show less enthusiasm for the war than did whites, and manifested somewhat greater reluctance to go overseas or to enter combat."[41] One group of young Blacks in Chicago formed a group called the "Conscientious Objectors Against Jim Crow" in 1941 and urged others to resist the draft because of the segregation in the armed forces.

The tenacity with which the armed forces maintained segregation, and the contortions it sometimes had to go through to coordinate the efforts of two separate armies — one white and one Black — suggested to many Blacks that the maintenance of segregation seemed more important to the army and the country as a whole than victory over the enemy.

Racial violence flared up at virtually every post in the United States and abroad when Black GIs tried to use the normally superior facilities alloted to white GIs — entertainment, post exchanges, etc. Race riots took place

*Black service troops line up at a segregated mess hall at an Army Air Corps base in Florida in 1943.*

*Above: Lieut. Gen. Mark Clark inspects a Black infantry unit in Italy in World War II.*
*Right: Members of the 25th Combat Team, 93rd Division, fording a stream in the South Pacific.*

*Above: Black GIs in Italy. Below: Black troops cleaning
weapons in the Pacific theater.*

at such places as Ft. Bragg, Camp Robinson, Camp Davis, Camp Lee, and Ft. Dix during the war.

Black doubts about the value of fighting a war between two white-supremacist countries were increased by widely publicized incidents in which Black GIs in the South were refused service at restaurants that willingly served German prisoners of war.

The growing shortage of manpower in 1943 led to a change in the army's policy towards Black units. Pressure to commit some Black combat units to battle began to build within the War Department in 1943. Additionally, a drastic shortage of infantry replacements as a result of the Battle of the Bulge in the winter of 1944-45 persuaded General Eisenhower that Black troops should be allowed to volunteer as infantry replacements in white companies. Those who did volunteer were assigned to white units and participated in the fighting in Germany in 1945.

Despite this partial integration, spurred by a critical need for manpower and reversed when the war ended, World War II marked a period when the Black mind and morale had been deeply shaken by the events and treatment accorded Blacks.

Black sociologist E. Franklin Frazier cites the war as the point where Blacks were no longer willing to accept discrimination without protest. Charles Silberman observes that the war marked a "turning point in American race relations" from which "the seeds of the protest movements of the 1950s and 1960s were sown." [42]

Blacks who served in the armed forces overseas during the war, more than 500,000 in all, also found that they were often better treated by the Europeans and Asians, including defeated enemy civilians, than they were by their white fellow GIs. This, too, only served to point out the contradictions of their position more graphically and dramatically.

Upon returning to the United States, Black veterans again faced all the discrimination that had existed when they left. They were denied equal opportunity for employment. They were less able to take advantage of G. I. mortgages due to housing segregation. They were less able to take advantage of the G. I. Bill than white veterans because they were less likely to have finished high school before the war.

After helping to defeat the "racist" regime of Adolf Hitler, the Black veteran returned to find the racist regime of the United States unvanquished.

Military leaders realized after World War II that the methods of utilizing Black manpower had not been satisfactory, and that in the postwar army changes were in order. It had been noticed that the morale and fighting qualities of those Blacks integrated into white units in 1945 had been higher than among Blacks restricted to segregated units.

Postwar pressure from Black protests to end segregation in the armed forces helped to speed the process of change. In 1948, A. Philip Randolph publicly advised all Blacks to "refuse to serve in the military until it was desegregated." In a confrontation with Senator Wayne Morse before a Senate Committee on April 12, 1948, Randolph stated that if America "does not develop the democratic process at home and make the . . . process work by giving the very people whom they propose to draft in the Army to fight for them democracy, democracy then is not the type of democracy that ought to be fought for. . . ."[43]

Randolph called for a campaign of civil disobedience as the "only way by which we are going to make America wake up and realize that we do not have democracy here as long as one Black man is denied all of the rights enjoyed by all the white men in this country."[44]

He argued that Blacks should serve a higher law than the law which punished them for refusal to serve in the armed forces when they were attempting to win democracy and make "the soul of America democratic."[45]

In 1948, President Truman ordered the full integration of the armed services. By the time the Korean War broke out in 1950, military integration was universal in policy although limited in practice.

Under this new policy, the color bar was removed from army jobs and schools, all racial quotas were abolished, including the former 10 percent ceiling on Blacks in the armed forces, and Blacks could now be assigned to any unit as their qualifications merited. Segregated units were still maintained but would presumably decline since Blacks no longer had to serve in them. In 1951, three years after the integration of the armed forces, there were still 200,000 Blacks in 385 all-Black units. In the course of the Korean War, however, the army, worried about the relatively poor performance and low morale of Blacks in segregated units, deactivated all Black units and assigned Blacks to previously white units. Before this order went into effect, however, one all-Black unit, the Twenty-fourth, captured Yech'on in the first United States victory of the war, and Private William H. Thompson, a unit member, became the first Afro-American to win a Congressional Medal of Honor since the Spanish-American War.

The results of the integration of the troops during the Korean war were dramatically clear. A group of social scientists studying the results concluded that Black soldiers performed better when not restricted to segregated units and that the effectiveness of the army was considerably enhanced by integration.

By the end of 1954, *de jure* segregation and discrimination were virtually eliminated from the internal structure of the active military forces, and equal treatment had become official military policy. In fact, the armed forces rapidly became the least segregated of the major institutions in American society. Off-post civilian communities, however, remained a constant reminder that the equality of Black soldiers was strictly limited to equality in the defense of American society and did not extend to participation as citizens.

Black veterans returning to the United States from Korea were constantly reminded of their inequality in education, employment, and in basic civil and human rights like the right to vote.

It is widely maintained that the United States armed services are the most integrated institutions in American society today. This may well be true, but it is fraught with irony. First, to say that something is the most integrated institution in American society does not mean it is not a racist institution. It simply means less racist than the rest of society. As the NAACP's Task Force Report on Administration of Military Justice stated in 1972, "systematic racial discrimination exists throughout the Armed Forces and in the Military Justice system. No command or installation and more important—no element of the military system — is entirely free from the effects of systematic discrimination against military servicemen as individuals and as groups."[46]

The Black Congressional Caucus also investigated racism in the military and found that Black troops:

1) received a disproportionately low number of honorable discharges and were more widely subject to pretrial confinement;

2) suffered harassment and intimidation for wearing Afro hairstyles or Black Power symbols;

3) failed to win key command posts over less qualified whites;

4) got the most dangerous combat jobs in Vietnam if they showed signs of Black militancy;

5) often received indifferent medical attention while in the field. [47]

The official report of a human relations team of the Air Force Air Training Command on conditions at fifteen air bases stated that "there is discrimination and racism in the command and it is ugly." They reported that at the bases they studied "unequal treatment is manifested in unequal punishment, offensive and inflammatory language, prejudice in the assignment of details, lack of products for Blacks in the BX [base exchange], harassment by security policemen under orders to break up five or more Blacks in a group, double standards in enforcement of regulations."[48]

Representative Parren Mitchell of Maryland concluded that "racism in the military is so deep, so wide and so effective that we can't possibly cope with it."[49]

The rise of Black nationalist sentiments in the Afro-

American population, and the growth of opposition to the war in Vietnam among all layers of this society have had the result of raising new questions about Black participation in the military adventures of the United States government. Black GIs have been less willing than ever to put up with the racism that still exists in the armed forces. And the fact that the armed forces are far more integrated than any other American institution, during an unpopular war, has not resulted in convincing the Black community that Blacks have a greater stake in American society because of this integration.

On the contrary, many Afro-Americans see this as a further indication of the hypocrisy of American society. The only place where Blacks even approach an even break in society is in a situation where they are given the "right" to serve in an increasingly unpopular military establishment and die in an unpopular war.

Young Blacks entering the armed forces bring with them the prevailing attitudes of their contemporaries and their peers. Being drafted does not have the effect of "wiping the slate clean." The young draftee or enlistee does not drop his previous attitudes and outlook.

The young Black serviceman, therefore, comes out of a situation in which there was a large majority sentiment in opposition to the war among Blacks and whites. Even though there are major divisions among Afro-Americans on most political and social questions, except the ultimate goal of full achievement of human and civil rights, there was a striking unanimity on the question of the war in Vietnam.

It is worthwhile looking at the reasons impelling Blacks as a whole to oppose the war in order to get a clearer understanding of the context in which Black GIs functioned.

Many groups and leaders who differed among themselves on strategic and tactical questions about how to win full human rights for Afro-Americans agreed on their opposition to the Vietnam War.

This unity of opposition to the war, despite differences on other questions, stemmed from the similarity of conclusions about the war. With the exception of the most conservative elements like Roy Wilkins and Whitney Young, all major Black leaders agreed on four major areas. All agreed that the stated war aims of the United States were hypocritical, that a bond of color existed between Black Americans and the yellow Vietnamese, that the United States was capable of commiting genocide against a nonwhite people, and that the war spending, when contrasted with spending to improve conditions of America's Black and white poor, illustrated the inhuman priorities of American society.

In previous wars, even wars that were unpopular among Black Americans as, for example, the crushing of the Filipino insurrection, the dominant attitude in Black communities was to use participation in the war to reenforce claims to equality and full citizenship. Participation was seen as providing an opportunity to demonstrate that Blacks had earned their rights to equality.

The attitudes on the Vietnam War were considerably different. A *Newsweek* magazine poll of Black attitudes on the war in 1969 pointed out that Blacks had come to regard Vietnam "as their own particular incubus — a war that depletes their young manhood and saps the resources available to healing their ills at home."50 In other words, rather than being a vehicle through which Blacks could gain benefits and full participation in society, the war was seen as an obstacle to improvements in their condition.

Between 1963 and 1969 *Newsweek* commissioned three Gallup polls on Black attitudes. The extent of the growth in opposition to American involvement in Southeast Asia could be seen by comparing the results of the polls. In 1966, 35 percent of the Black population opposed the war because they had less freedom in the United States. By 1969, this 35 percent minority had become a "56-31 majority sentiment." One out of seven Black Americans in 1969 did not even "consider the United States worth fighting for in a world war."

The gap between the American ideal and the reality

of Black people's conditions in the United States is one of the Afro-American's strongest grievances. Malcolm X frequently contrasted the "American dream" with the Black "American nightmare." As a result of this country's failure to deliver on its stated democratic ideals, Afro-Americans developed tremendous skepticism and cynicism regarding the government's rhetoric about "defending democracy" and fighting for the self-determination of a small country. Having experienced American-style "democracy" first hand, many Afro-Americans could deeply sympathize with the resistance of the Vietnamese to its imposition on them. As Malcolm X put it, "You and I haven't benefited from America's democracy, we've only suffered from America's hypocrisy."

There is no system in the world that has proven itself "more corrupt, more criminal" than the American system of democracy that "still enslaves twenty-two million Afro-Americans," Malcolm told the Militant Labor Forum in New York in April 1964. He denounced the hypocrisy of a system that "can go all over this earth telling other people how to straighten out their house, when you have citizens of this country who have to use bullets if they want to cast a ballot."[51]

Malcolm X was one of the first Black leaders to speak out against American involvement in Vietnam. Speaking to a group of Black teenagers from McComb, Mississippi, on December 31, 1964, he blasted the United States as having "the most hypocritical government since the world began" because it was "supposed to be a democracy, supposed to be for freedom and all of that kind of stuff when they want to draft you and put you in the army and send you to Saigon to fight for them — and then you've got to turn around and all night long discuss how you're going to just get a right to register and vote without being murdered."[52]

The Kennedy, Johnson, and Nixon administrations repeated time and again that America had an obligation to uphold the "rights" of its allies. Blacks were often quick to notice the contrast between this zeal and the fact that

"twenty-two million people are living witnesses to the fact
that America has failed to keep its constitutional commitment to its own Negro citizens at home."[53]

The government was willing to send more than half
a million GIs to "defend democracy" in South Vietnam.
But at the height of the voter registration drives in the
South, after widespread intimidation and murders of
Blacks trying to register, less than two hundred federal
marshals and registrars could be found for assignment

to Mississippi, Alabama, South Carolina, and elsewhere, although it was the president's sworn duty to uphold the constitutional rights of citizens of this country. As novelist John Oliver Killens put it: "We Black folk find it difficult to understand the nation's hesitation about sending troops to Mississippi to guarantee free elections when we read of American boys dying thousands of miles from home to ensure freedom for the Vietnamese. The subtlety escapes us."[54]

During the height of the civil rights movement, when the government and political leaders continually admonished Blacks to remain nonviolent, to avoid striking back at those who beat and murdered them, Black youth were being drafted into the army to engage in violence against the Vietnamese people. The hypocrisy of the government's stance was clear to many, but it was Malcolm X, again, who gave this realization its most biting expression:

> Look right now what's going on in and around Saigon and Hanoi and in the Congo and elsewhere. They are violent when their interests are at stake. But for all that violence they display at the international level, when you and I want just a little bit of freedom, we're supposed to be nonviolent. They're violent in Korea, they're violent in Germany, they're violent in the South Pacific, they're violent in Cuba, they're violent wherever they go. But when it comes time for you and me to protect ourselves against lynchings, they tell us to be nonviolent.[55]

Furthermore, Malcolm X understood and exposed the powerful dynamic that was being set in motion by the white man's military necessities. "How are you going to be nonviolent in Mississippi, as violent as you were in Korea?" he asks—for the combination of the war and the civil rights movement had posed moral questions in a new way for Black Americans: "If it is wrong to be violent defending Black women and Black children . . . then it is wrong for America to draft us and make us violent

67

abroad in defense of her. And if it is right for America to draft us, and teach us how to be violent in defense of her, then it is right for you and me to do whatever is necessary to defend our own people right here in this country."[56]

He called on his fellow Afro-Americans to stop "walking around in America, getting ready to be drafted and sent abroad, like a tin soldier."[57]

Because of the obvious disparity between the stated goals of the United States in Vietnam and the commitment towards those same goals in the United States, it should not surprise anyone that the first organized civil rights group to protest the Vietnam war was a group in the deep South that had had first-hand experience with the lack of federal protection for Blacks trying to exercise basic democratic rights.

This first organized protest took the form of a leaflet circulated in McComb, Mississippi, and printed in the Mississippi Freedom Democratic Party newsletter of McComb on July 28, 1965. The statement said, in part: "It is very easy to understand why Negro citizens of McComb, themselves the victims of bombings, Klan-inspired terrorism, and harassment arrests, should resent the death of a citizen of McComb while fighting in Vietnam for 'freedom' not enjoyed by the Negro community of McComb."[58]

The leaflet had been circulated after the death of John D. Shaw, 23, of McComb, who had been a participant in civil rights demonstrations there in 1961. It gave the following reasons why Blacks should not fight any war for America. First, no Mississippi Blacks should fight in Vietnam for the white man's freedom until all Black people were free in Mississippi. Second, Blacks would gain respect as a race by forcing the American government and the Mississippi government to come with guns, dogs, and trucks to take them away to fight and be killed. Finally, no one had a right to ask Blacks to risk their lives in Vietnam so that white Americans could get richer.

Although Malcolm X had spoken out against the war from its very inception, the first protest by a national civil rights group came on January 6, 1966, when the Student Non-violent Coordinating Committee (SNCC) announced its opposition. The statement received wide attention, especially after it was endorsed by SNCC's then communications director, Julian Bond, who had just been elected to the Georgia House of Representatives. When Bond refused to repudiate SNCC's criticism of the war, he was termed "disloyal" by some legislators, and was expelled by the legislature, although he was later seated as a result of a Supreme Court ruling.

SNCC opposed the war on the grounds that the United States government was deceptive in its claims of concern for the freedom of the Vietnamese people just as it was deceptive in its claims of concern for the freedom of Blacks in the United States itself.

Field work, particularly in the South, had revealed to SNCC workers that the United States government never guaranteed freedom to Black citizens and was not yet truly determined to "end the rule of terror . . . within its own borders." The statement concluded that "we support the men . . . who are unwilling to respond to the military draft which would compel them to contribute their lives to U. S. aggression in the name of the 'freedom' we find so false in this country. . . . We take note . . . that 16 percent of the draftees are Negroes, called on . . . to preserve a 'democracy' which does not exist for them at home."[59]

Several months later, in April 1966, the Southern Christian Leadership Conference, led by Dr. Martin Luther King, also adopted a strong resolution on the war at a time when the Buddhist revolt was being crushed by the Ky government in South Vietnam. The staff of CORE became open in its criticisms of the war after the appointment of Floyd McKissick as its national chairman in 1965.

The war had an especially powerful impact on the political perspectives of Black youth. In October 1966, the Black Panther Party issued its ten point program. Point six declared: "We want all Black men to be exempt from military service." The rationale for the demand was: "We believe that Black people should not be forced to fight in the military service to defend a racist government that does not protect us. We will not fight and kill other people of color in the world who, like Black people, are being victimized by the white racist government of America."[60]

There was a certain historical parallel between the attitude of Black Americans to the crushing of the Filipino insurrection and their attitude to the attempt to crush the Vietnamese revolution. Since both wars were fought against nonwhite populations, and in an extremely brutal manner, many Blacks felt a sense of identification with the "enemy" in both instances.

One SNCC field worker put it this way: "You know, I just saw one of those Vietcong guerrillas on TV. He was dark-skinned, ragged, poor, and angry. I swear, he looked just like one of us."[61]

Julius Williams, the NAACP's national director for Armed Services and Veteran Affairs made a similar point in 1972, saying: "It's an unpopular war and the Black who goes over and fights isn't looked upon as a hero. It's not just society but his own people who feel that the war is only making Black people kill brown people."[62]

This feeling of identity is built on a number of points. First, many Blacks see Black America as a nation colonized by white America, just as Africa, Latin America, and Asia are colonized by white Europeans and Americans. Second, for those worried about Black survival as a minority in the United States, international solidarity with other nonwhite peoples around the world offers a source of strength and potential allies. Third, Blacks, being a nonwhite *minority* in a world with a nonwhite *majority* gain a sense of strength from the fact that they share a basic kinship with the majority of the world. Seen from that perspective, the white race — which now has its foot on their neck, and on the necks of other nonwhite peoples around the world — is actually a small minority on the planet, a minority that will be hard-pressed to maintain its hegemony in the face of a united majority.

The broadening of Black perspectives to include the rest of the world outside the United States has been a feature

70

*Many Blacks opposed use of Black GIs in Vietnam.*
*This GI is bringing in a 17-year-old woman captured*
*in a raid on an NLF training base.*

*GIs commemorate Dr. Martin Luther King Jr.'s birthday in Long Binh, Vietnam, 1971.*

that has marked the evolution of virtually all tendencies in the Black liberation movement.

Malcolm X, in this as in so many other ways a forerunner of the rest of the movement, saw the need to strengthen the Afro-American struggle for human rights in the United States by forging an alliance with the colored masses of the world, by internationalizing the Afro-American problem, by making it not simply a Black problem or an American problem, but, as he often stated, "a world problem, a problem for humanity."

In identifying with all colonial revolutions, he held that anyone who caught the same kind of hell he did was his brother. Oppression, exploitation, degradation, discrimination, segregation, humiliation forged a link between them. They shared a common oppressor and enemy — white Western society.

Malcolm, in his later years especially, was careful to dispell the notion that he was against whites as whites. He argued that he was "for anybody who's for freedom. I'm for anybody who's for justice . . . equality. I'm not for anybody who tells me to sit around and wait for mine . . . who tells me to turn the other cheek . . . who tells Black people to be nonviolent while nobody is telling white people to be nonviolent."63

During the civil war in the Congo, when white mercenaries and United Nations forces were intervening from two different directions to crush Patrice Lumumba's movement, Malcolm pointed out that the same interests, the same sides, the same schemes were at work there and in Mississippi. Blacks would be "out of our minds," he said, and "would actually be traitors to ourselves, to be reluctant or fearful to identify with people" with whom we have so much in common. "When you have people who look exactly like you, and you are catching hell to boot, and you still are reluctant or hesitant or slow to identify with them, then you need to catch hell. . . . You deserve all the hell you get."64

Wherever nonwhite people were being oppressed or exploited, Malcolm believed that Blacks had reason to get together with them on the basis of their common enemy. Joint activity and support among all the oppressed masses in Asia, Africa, Latin America, and North America would build a powerful base that would work for the benefit of all of them. One month before his assassination, he continued to link the problem of racism in Mississippi with racism in South Vietnam. In a radio interview he argued that the Vietnam war was part of the racist system used by Western powers to degrade people in Asia in recent centuries. His expressed hope was that the Afro-American would see that his problem was the same as the problem of people being oppressed by the United States and its allies in Southeast Asia.

Dr. Martin Luther King's view also broadened to include oppressed people outside the United States. As the winner of the Nobel Peace Prize in 1964, Dr. King felt he had an obligation to speak out against oppression everywhere in the world. He wrote that no matter how deeply the Black American was involved with being free in America, Blacks could not ignore "the larger world house in which we are also dwellers." He argued that "what is happening in the United States today is a significant part of a world development," the development of a "worldwide freedom revolution."

"All over the world like a fever freedom is spreading in the widest liberation movement in history. The great masses of people are determined to end the exploitation of their races and lands. They are awake and moving toward their goal like a tidal wave. . . . Oppressed people cannot remain oppressed forever. The yearning for freedom eventually manifests itself."[65]

Before his assassination, King began to play a major role in the antiwar movement, lending his authority to its activities and speaking at mass rallies.

Many other Black activists have acknowledged the identity between the Vietnamese and Afro-American liberation struggles. Bobby Seale of the Black Panther Party traced the connection in this way: "The Vietnamese have had political decisions made upon them and their country and they have disagreed with them. So, they said, Naw, we're going to defend ourselves right here on our land, and we want you to withdraw from our land. Now, we . . . parallel the situation, when we see all these racist cops off in our community the way they are. . . . they occupy our community just like a foreign troop occupying territory."66

Similarly, Julius Lester, poet, folksinger, former SNCC worker, invokes the identity of the Afro-American with the oppressed of the world on the basis that "his blackness links him with the Indians of Peru, the miners in Bolivia, the African and the freedom fighters of Vietnam. What they fight for is what the American Black man fights for — the right to govern his own life."67

In the same spirit, Stokely Carmichael draws the connection between Afro-Americans and others fighting American imperialism. America, he says, is an "octopus of exploitation," whose tentacles stretch "from Mississippi and Harlem to . . . the Middle East . . . and Vietnam; the form varies from area to area but the essential result has been the same — a powerful few have been maintained and enriched at the expense of the poor and voiceless colored masses."68

Therefore, he concludes, it is essential for Blacks to forge alliances with liberation struggles around the world, alliances that will strengthen both parties.

Eldridge Cleaver observed, in *Soul on Ice,* that Afro-Americans are "asked to die for the System in Vietnam" while they are killed by the same system in Watts. Rather than go to Vietnam, he asked, "why not die right here in Babylon fighting for a better life, like the Viet Cong?" 69

The possibility that white America may be considering genocide against the Afro-American population is more widely accepted in the Black community than most white Americans realize. Few Blacks deny that America is at least capable of genocide. The historical mistreatment and neglect of American Indians, Japanese-Americans, Chinese-Americans, dark-skinned Latins and all other nonwhites in this country is eloquent testimony to the depth of racist sentiments and practice in American history.

For two and a half centuries Black Americans were held in slavery, were regarded as nonhuman or sub-human. As Martin Luther King pointed out, racism has its logical extension in genocide. When a group feels that another group is condemned by nature to hereditary inferiority, when there is acceptance of the notion that "one race has carried progress throughout human history and can alone ensure future progress," then the ultimate logic is to assume that "the hope of civilization depends upon eliminating some races and keeping others pure."[70] In this context, few Black Americans have any doubt which race would be eliminated and which kept pure.

King asserted that if white America says that a Black man, because of his race, is not good enough to have a job equal to his, or to attend school with him, or to live next door to him, the white man is by implication stating that "that man does not deserve to exist" because his existence is "corrupt and defective."

The United States has traditionally adopted two standards for action on any question, depending on whether whites or nonwhites are involved. During World War II, for example, Japanese-Americans were thrown into concentration camps because the United States was at war with Japan, while German-Americans and Italian-Americans were never considered for similar treatment.

Similarly, during World War II the United States twice used atomic bombs on Japan. Gwendolyn Patton echoes the feelings of many Black Americans when she asks why this country dropped the bomb on Japan, "a yellow nation, and not on Germany, the initiator of World War II?" Her conclusion was that Japan, as a nonwhite nation, could be used by the United States as a testing ground for the new weapon, in the same way that another nonwhite nation, Vietnam, was the testing ground for the massive use of such weapons as chemical defoliants.[71]

While few Black Americans would assert that America is now preparing for genocide against Afro-Americans in the same way Hitler applied it to Jews, throughout the course of the Vietnam war Blacks were quick to point out that their youth were being used as cannon fodder and were suffering proportionally more casualties than white youth. By a margin of two to one, according to the *Newsweek* polls, Black Americans felt that "their young are fighting a disproportionate share of the war."[72]

These sentiments were substantiated by the figures on Black participation in Vietnam. During the 1960s, proportionally more Blacks (30 percent) than whites (18 percent) from the draft-qualified age group were drafted. While Blacks were generally no more than 11 percent of the total enlisted personnel in Vietnam, they comprised nearly 15 percent of all army units, and in army combat units the proportion was appreciably higher. In terms of casualties, Blacks suffered nearly 17 percent of all deaths in Vietnam between 1961 and 1967 although the percentage of Black troops in Southeast Asia during those years was around 12 percent. In 1970, while they were 11 percent of the troops in Vietnam, Blacks took 22 percent of the casualties.

Dr. Martin Luther King used the Black participation in Vietnam to point out one of the ironies of American life: that Blacks have half as much of the good things as whites, and twice as much of the bad things.

Thus, said King: "half of all Negroes live in substandard housing, and Negroes have half the income of whites. . . . There are twice as many unemployed. The rate of infant mortality . . . is double that of whites."

This proportion also applied to the war. King pointed to the fact that "there were twice as many Negroes as whites in combat in Vietnam at the beginning of 1967, and twice as many Negro soldiers died in action (20.6 percent) in proportion to their numbers in the population."[73]

The Black community in the United States was also very sensitive to charges that Blacks were being forced to take on the most dangerous assignments within combat units, that they were being sacrificed. Reports of mistreatment and discrimination were reflected in letters to the editors of Black publications from servicemen in Vietnam. One Black PFC pointed out: "You should see for yourself how the Black man is being treated over here. And the way we are dying. When it comes to rank we are left out. When it comes to special privileges we are left out. When it come to patrols . . . we are first."[74]

Another letter reads in part: "When a 'brother' speaks out against the unequal treatment . . . he is most assuredly 'railroaded' to the D.M.Z. [Demilitarized zone], An Khe or some other extremely dangerous area."[75]

The vulnerability of the Black soldier in Vietnam was described by David Parks who kept a daily chronicle of his experiences as a combat soldier and published these in a book entitled *GI Diary*. One entry taken from January 31, 1967, says: "The odds are against him. Sgt. Paulson handpicks the men for this job. So far, it seems to me he's fingered only Negroes and Puerto Ricans. I think he's trying to tell us something. . . . I get the feeling that I should have been born white. . . . If only the souls and Puerto Ricans could tell the world what really happens to them in this man's Army."[76]

Thornell Grant, a veteran who had spent his time in Vietnam driving an ammunition truck, told the *Boston Globe* that "one thing about Black soldiers in Vietnam is that a lot of them die." He added that "you don't find many of them getting their stripes when they are supposed to or receiving medals but you see them wounded or lying in a ditch somewhere and you know good and well the man don't care."[77]

Using Blacks in Vietnam was, according to one Black twenty-five-year-old who refused to serve in the U.S. armed forces, nothing more than using "nigger against chink."[78]

Others have spoken of the possibility of genocide in more explicit terms. Eldridge Cleaver, for example, spoke of the connection of U.S. policies in Vietnam with treatment of Afro-Americans. "The American racial problem," he stated, "can no longer be spoken of . . . in isolation. The relationship between the genocide in Vietnam and the smiles of the white man toward Black Americans is a direct relationship. Once the white man solves his problems in the East he will then turn . . . on the Black people of America, his longtime punching bag."[79]

Cleaver felt that it was no accident "that the United States government is sending all those Black troops to Vietnam." The government's purpose, he maintained, was "to kill off the cream of Black youth" by sending "16 percent Black troops to Vietnam."[80] Less categorical, but making the same point, was the comment of Ron Brown, a young Black GI in Vietnam who observed that "in my mind Vietnam has killed a lot of young Blacks in this country, eliminating them, as if the war was a plan to do so."[81]

The Vietnam War, probably more than any other single event in decades, demonstrated to Black Americans that the reason for their lack of material progress was not so much this society's lack of financial and material resources to improve housing, education, and job opportunities as its lack of willingness to *commit* the resources to those uses.

The government's prosecution of the war at the cost of tens of billions of dollars a year, and its willingness to ultimately invest the manpower of several million GIs to carry it out, showed that the resources were indeed available. But it also showed that the government was willing to mobilize these resources to kill National Liberation Front fighters in Vietnam, to bomb the countryside of North and South Vietnam, to burn villages, defoliate crops and forests, to take many innocent lives, and to create millions of refugees, while it was not willing to mobilize those resources to replace slum housing or improve ghetto education.

By 1969, according to the previously cited *Newsweek* poll, Blacks were already persuaded by a margin of seven to one that "Vietnam is directly pinching the home-front war on poverty."

In a very basic sense, the massive opposition of Afro-Americans to U.S. policy in Vietnam reflected the growth of cynicism about American society. Old rationales no longer were taken as good coin. Earlier feelings that if Blacks could only prove themselves American society would open up to them were replaced by a feeling that American society was not closed to them out of misunder-

79

standing but through conscious policy. Perhaps the most succinct expression of the cynicism about the United States was contained in the comment of one Afro-American who was heavily involved in the civil rights struggle in Mississippi. "Our criticism of Vietnam policy," he said, "does not come from what we know of Vietnam, but from what we know of America."[82]

The widespread opposition of Afro-Americans to the Vietnam war and their unwillingness to accept manifestations of racism in the armed forces resulted in much disaffection among Black GIs. As a 1971 NAACP report stated, "an uncomfortable number of young Black servicemen are disenchanted, alienated and have lost faith in the capacity and the will of the armed forces to deal honestly with their problems."[83]

This lack of faith in the capacity and willingness of the armed forces to change the prevailing racism led GIs to feel that they themselves must protest against racism and act against it. The common oppression of Blacks forged a tremendous bond between them in Vietnam. As one Black GI put it: "In Vietnam, whenever you saw a brother and gave him the power sign he gave it right back."[84]

There was little feeling among the troops that their own demands for equality should be subordinated to the war effort. This was especially true since most GIs, Black and white, did not feel that the war had anything to do with their interests. As Aaron Cross, a young Black GI observed: "I didn't want to go to Vietnam. I didn't think I had anything to fight for. I don't think anyone knew why I was over there. . . . I often wondered what they would have told my parents if I had been killed. That I died for my country?"[85]

The new spirit of the Black GIs often threw their white officers into a panic. Officers in Vietnam began to develop a paranoic fear of giving direct orders to Afro-American GIs for fear of getting "fragged." The number of actual cases of "fragging," throwing a fragmentation grenade into an officer's tent, was probably exaggerated. But enough cases did take place to keep many officers on

*Two GIs in Germany salute an officer.*

edge. And the practice was not restricted to Black GIs. White GIs in Vietnam, who were also affected by anti-war sentiment at home and by a realization that the war had nothing to do with their interests, also engaged in the practice.

But much more significant than fragging was the development of organized groups resisting racism and opposing the war in the armed forces. These groups probably reached their high point in 1970 in Germany. General Michael S. Davison, the commander of the Seventh Army, acknowledged that in that year "Black dissident organizations could turn out 1500 soldiers for a demonstration."[86] It is estimated that there were twenty such organizations in ten cities in Germany. These groups held rallies and protest marches and published underground newspapers. Some of their activities were coordinated with German radical student groups, like the July 4, 1970, rally at the University of Heidelberg attended by over 1000 GIs, most of them Black.

Perhaps the action by Black GIs in Germany that most embarrassed the army was a petition signed by over 100 Black GIs from the Berlin area, 60 from Frankfurt, and 56 from Darmstad addressed to Soviet and East German authorities asking them, as parties with some say over the international administration of West Berlin, to act against the discrimination against Black GIs in West Berlin by the American and West German authorities.

Organized activity, however, was not restricted to Germany. In the United States there were also numerous demonstrations, rallies, and groups formed by Black and white GIs. One of the earliest of such occurences was the case of the Fort Hood 43. In August 1968, at the time of the Chicago Democratic National Convention, units at Fort Hood, Texas, were put on alert for possible use in Chicago for "riot control" duty. Several hundred Black GIs gathered to protest this assignment, and forty-three were arrested and court martialed.

In early 1969, Black GIs at Fort Jackson, South Carolina, organized an antiwar group called GIs United Against the War in Vietnam. It was organized by a Black GI, Joe Miles, a member of the Young Socialist Alliance and Socialist Workers Party. Miles began GIs United by playing tape recordings of Malcolm X's speeches in his barracks. GIs United later expanded its membership to white antiwar GIs as well as Blacks, Puerto Ricans, and Chicanos. From January to May 1969 GIs United was able to hold regular meetings of fifty or more GIs on base. In May, the army arrested eight of the leaders of the group and placed them in the stockade. Due to a national defense campaign, however, the Army was unable to successfully court-martial the GIs, and charges against them were dropped. [87]

At Fort McClellan, Alabama, on November 15, 1971, seventy-one Black GIs and sixty-eight Black WACs were arrested after a series of demonstrations and mass meetings on post opposing racial discrimination. Most eventually had the charges against them dropped or were discharged from the armed forces.

But it was in the navy that some of the most dramatic incidents involving Blacks took place. The navy has had the smallest percentage of Blacks of any of the services, with only 6.9 percent of the enlisted men, 4 percent of the noncommissioned officers, and 0.9 percent of the officers being Afro-Americans.

Two of the largest incidents in the navy took place in the same week in October 1972 on the aircraft carriers *Kitty Hawk* and *Constellation*. On the *Kitty Hawk,* fights between Black and white seamen lasted for fifteen hours and resulted in the hospitalization of forty whites and six Blacks.

Four days later, racial turmoil resulted in the cancellation of a training exercise on the *Constellation* and forced the ship to return to port. Upon arriving in port, 122 Black sailors and 8 white sailors staged a dockside sitdown, raised clenched fist salutes, and refused to reboard the vessel.

Within a month of these two incidents, clashes were reported between Blacks and whites aboard the assault ship *USS Sumpter* and a battle took place on the *USS Hassayampa* in the Philippines. Major battles on Midway Island and in Norfolk, Virginia, took place a month later.

In all these incidents, 196 men, almost all Black, were arrested. Of these, 147 received "non-judicial punishment," and 15 had charges dropped or were found not guilty.

These clashes were the result of the Black sailors' unwillingness to accept racist insults, and their protest against the discrimination in assignments and promotions in the Navy.

In conclusion, history indicates that white America generally restricted Black participation in the armed forces until emergency situations forced the use of Black manpower. But, at the same time, the Black American traditionally viewed his military record as proof of his loyalty and as a claim to full citizenship. Seeking participation in America's wars, he held the hope that his sacrifices would bring the reward of increased rights to America's biggest minority. It was this optimism that had been one of the major factors behind his loyalty from the Revolutionary War to Korea.

But even as early as 1766, some Blacks counseled that it was inconsistent for them to fight for American independence while the country adhered to the tenets of slavery. In later wars this sentiment was expressed in terms of an unwillingness to forget that the real enemy was at home in America.

At the end of each war, Black veterans returned to their inferior status in American society, either as slaves or as separate and unequal citizens, the recipients of inferior education, the worst jobs, and white violence, North and South.

During the course of the Vietnam war, the majority of Afro-Americans and most Afro-American political groups opposed the war, seeing it as a waste of Black youth, a waste of resources that could be better used to ameliorate the conditions of America's poor, and often

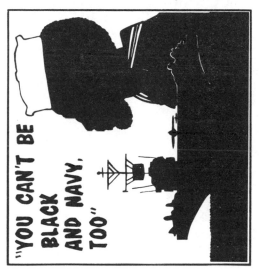

"YOU CAN'T BE BLACK AND NAVY, TOO"

*Two views
of Blacks
and the
U. S. Navy.*

**FREE THE KITTY HAWK 21**
**BLACK SERVICEMEN'S CAUCUS**

3109 IMPERIAL AVE.   SAN DIEGO   CALIF.  –  PHONE  233–1893

**DONATIONS**

ARE NEEDED FOR THE DEFENSE COMMITTEE

# You can be Black, and Navy too.

a racist war against a colored people struggling for self-determination.

For the first time, the great majority of Blacks, inside and outside the military, were unwilling to defer their demands until the end of the war. They felt they did not have to *prove* their right to citizenship through military service, but rather that they should not be forced to fight and possibly die for a society unwilling to grant them full civil and human rights.

# NOTES

1. Richard M. Dalfiume, *Desegregation of the U.S. Armed Forces,* University of Missouri Press, 1969, pp. 1-5.
2. John Hope Franklin, *From Slavery to Freedom,* Random House, 1969, pp. 127-128.
3. *Ibid.,* p. 133.
4. *Ibid.*
5. Martin R. Delany, *The Condition, Elevation, Emigration, and Destiny of the Colored People of the United States,* Arno Press, 1969, p. 73.
6. Franklin, p. 168.
7. Full text of proclamation in *Correspondence of Andrew Jackson,* Vol. II, edited by John S. Bassett, Carnegie Institute of Washington, 1927, pp. 58-59.
8. Delany, p. 78.
9. "Address to the Troops in New Orleans; to the Men of Color," in *Correspondence of Andrew Jackson,* pp. 118-119.
10. Dalfiume, p. 6.
11. Frederick Douglass, "The Proclamation and a Negro Army," full text in *The Life and Writings of Frederick Douglas,* Vol. III, edited by Philip S. Foner, International Publishers, 1952, pp. 334-336.
12. "Men of Color to Arms!" in *ibid.,* pp. 317-319.
13. *Ibid.*
14. "Why Should a Colored Man Enlist?" in *ibid.,* pp. 340-344.
15. Address at National Hall, Philadelphia, July 6, 1863, in *ibid.,* p. 365.
16. Rudolf J. Friederich, "54 Black Heroes: Medal of Honor Winners," *Crisis* magazine, June-July 1969, p. 243.
17. Franklin, pp. 293-294.
18. W.E.B. Du Bois, *Black Reconstruction,* S.A. Russell Co., 1956, p. 107.
19. Delany, p. 48.
20. *Ibid.,* pp. 48-51.
21. *Ibid.,* p. 51.
22. *Ibid.,* p. 67.
23. H.T. Kealing, "The Characteristics of the Negro People," in *The Negro Problem,* Arno Press, 1969, pp. 167-170.
24. *Ibid.,* pp. 170-171.
25. T. Thomas Fortune, "The Negro's Place in American Life at the Present Day," in *ibid.,* p. 223.
26. Addison Gayle, Jr., *The Black Situation,* Horizon Press, 1970, p. 93.

27. Willard B. Gatewood, Jr., *Smoked Yankees,* University of Illinois Press, 1971, p. 10.
28. *Ibid.,* p. 13
29. Stephen Bonsal, "The Negro Soldier in War and Peace," *North American Review* (186), June 1907, pp. 325-326.
30. Charles C. Moskos, Jr., "Racial Integration in the Armed Forces," in *The Making of Black America,* Vol. II, edited by August Meier and Elliot Rudwick, Atheneum Press, 1969, p. 437.
31. "These Truly are the Brave," *Ebony* magazine, August 1968, p. 173.
32. Dalfiume, p. 9.
33. *Ibid.*
34. *Ibid.,* p. 10.
35. Gayle, p. 94.
36. *Ibid.*
37. *Crisis* magazine, pp. 13-14.
38. Claude McKay, "Harlem Shadows," in *Black Voices,* edited by Abraham Chapman, Mentor Books, 1968, p. 372.
39. Editorial entitled "Returning Soldiers," *Crisis* magazine, May 1919, p. 14.
40. Dalfiume, p. 131.
41. David G. Mandelbaum, *Soldier Groups and Negro Soldiers,* University of California Press, 1952, p. 95.
42. Cited by Dalfiume, pp. 103-106.
43. *Congressional Record,* XCIV (April 12, 1948), p. 4312.
44. *Ibid.,* p. 4313.
45. *Ibid.*
46. Cited in *Jet* magazine, December 2, 1971.
47. Cited in *Time* magazine, November 29, 1971.
48. *New York Times,* August 31, 1971.
49. *Time* magazine, November 29, 1971.
50. *Newsweek* magazine, June 30, 1969.
51. Malcolm X, "The Black Revolution," in *Malcolm X Speaks,* edited by George Breitman, Grove Press, 1965.
52. In *ibid.,* p. 144.
53. C. E. Wilson, "A Negro Looks at the War in Vietnam," *Liberator* magazine, March 1966, p. 32.
54. John O. Killens, *Black Man's Burden,* Pocket Books, 1969, p. 23.
55. *Malcolm X Speaks,* pp. 163-164.
56. *Ibid.,* pp. 7-8.
57. *Ibid.,* p. 35.

58. "The War on Vietnam," in *Black Protest,* edited by Joanne Grant, Fawcett Publications, 1968, p. 415.
59. "SNCC Statement on Vietnam, January 6, 1966," in *ibid.*
60. *The Black Panther,* June 13, 1970.
61. Howard Zinn, *Vietnam: The Logic of Withdrawal,* Beacon Press, 1967, p. 19.
62. *Boston Globe,* June 18, 1972.
63. *Malcolm X Speaks,* p. 112.
64. *Ibid.,* p. 130.
65. Martin Luther King, Jr., *Where Do We Go From Here: Chaos or Community?,* Bantam Books, 1968, p. 198.
66. Bobby Seale, "Free Huey," in *Rhetoric of Black Revolution,* Arthur L. Smith, Allyn and Bacon, 1969, p. 184.
67. Julius Lester, "The Angry Children of Malcolm X," printed in a pamphlet by the Southern Student Organizing Committee, 1966, p. 9.
68. Stokely Carmichael, "Power and Racism," printed in a pamphlet by the Southern Student Organizing Committee, 1969, p. 4.
69. Eldridge Cleaver, *Soul on Ice,* Delta Books, 1968, p. 137.
70. King, p. 82.
71. Gwendolyn Patton, "Black People and War," *Liberator* magazine, February 1967.
72. *Newsweek* magazine, June 30, 1969.
73. King, pp. 7-8.
74. Letters to the Editor, *Ebony* magazine, August 1968.
75. *Ibid.*
76. Cited in "The Black Man and the Draft," in *ibid.*
77. *Boston Globe,* June 18, 1972.
78. Rolland Snellings, "Vietnam; Whitey: I Will Not Serve," in *Liberator* magazine, March 1966.
79. Cleaver, p. 123.
80. *Ibid.,* p. 122.
81. *Boston Globe,* June 18, 1972.
82. Quoted by Zinn, p. 24.
83. *Jet* magazine, December 12, 1971.
84. *Boston Globe,* June 18, 1972.
85. *Ibid.*
86. *Christian Science Monitor,* February 3, 1972.
87. The case of the Fort Jackson 8 was the subject of a book by Fred Halstead, *GIs Speak Out Against the War,* Pathfinder Press, 1970.

Aptheker, Herbert. *The American Revolution: 1763-1783.* New York: International Publishers, 1960.

——. *The Negro in the Civil War.* New York: International Publishers, 1938.

Barbour, Floyd B., ed. *The Black Power Revolt.* Toronto: Collier-Macmillan Co., 1968.

Basler, Roy P., ed. *The Collected Works of Abraham Lincoln.* Vol. VI. New Brunswick, New Jersey: Rutgers University Press, 1953.

Bassett, John S., ed. *Correspondence of Andrew Jackson.* Vol. II. Washington, D.C.: Carnegie Institution of Washington, 1927.

Breitman, George, ed. *Malcolm X Speaks.* New York: Grove Press, 1965.

Cleaver, Eldridge. *Soul on Ice.* Delta Books. New York: Dell Publishing Co., 1968.

Dalfiume, Richard M. *Desegregation of the United States Armed Forces.* Missouri: University of Missouri Press, 1969.

Delany, Martin R. *The Condition, Elevation, Emigration, and Destiny of the Colored People of the United States.* New York: Arno Press, 1969.

Drake, St. Clair. "Folk and Classways Within the Black Ghetto." *The Making of Black America.* Edited by August Meier and Elliot Rudwick. Vol. II. New York: Atheneum Press, 1969.

Eaton, Clement. *A History of the South.* 2nd ed. New York: The Macmillan Co., 1966.

Fanon, Frantz. *The Wretched of the Earth.* Translated by Constance Farrington. New York: Grove Press, 1968.

Fishel, Jr., Leslie H., and Quarles, Benjamin, eds. *The Black American: A Documentary History.* New York: William Morrow and Co., 1970.

Foner, Philip S. *The Life and Writings of Frederick Douglass.* Vol. III. New York: International Publishers, 1952.

——. *W.E.B. Du Bois Speaks, Speeches and Addresses 1890-1919.* New York: Pathfinder Press, 1970.

——. *W.E.B. Du Bois Speaks, Speeches and Addresses 1920-1963.* New York: Pathfinder Press, 1970.

Franklin, John Hope. *From Slavery to Freedom.* Vintage Books. 3rd ed. New York: Random House, 1969.

Gatewood, Jr., Willard B. *Smoked Yankees.* Urbana: University of Illinois Press, 1971.

Gayle, Jr., Addison. *The Black Situation.* New York: Horizon Press, 1970.

Goldston, Robert. *The Negro Revolution.* New York: The Macmillan Co., 1968.

Grant, Joanne, ed. *Black Protest: History, Documents, and Analysis, 1619 to the Present.* Fawcett Premier Books. New York: Fawcett Publications, 1968.

Halstead, Fred. *GIs Speak Out Against the War, The Case of the Ft. Jackson 8.* New York: Pathfinder Press, 1970.

Killens, John O. *Black Man's Burden.* New York: Pocket Books, 1969.

King, Martin Luther. *Where Do We Go From Here: Chaos or Community?* Bantam Books. New York: Harper and Row, 1968.

Laue, James H. "The Changing Character of Negro Protest." *Black Revolt: Strategies of Protest.* Edited by Doris Y. Wilkinson. Berkeley: McCutchan Publishing Corp., 1969.

Lincoln, C. Eric. *The Black Muslims in America.* Boston: Beacon Press, 1961.

Mandelbaum, David G. *Soldier Groups and Negro Soldiers.* Berkeley: University of California Press, 1952.

McPherson, James M. *The Negro's Civil War.* Vintage Books. New York: Random House, 1967.

Meier, August, and Rudwick, Elliott, eds. *Black Protest in the Sixties.* Chicago: Quadrangle Books, 1970.

Moskos, Jr., Charles C. "Racial Integration in the Armed Forces." *The Making of Black America.* Edited by August Meier and Elliott Rudwick. Vol. II. New York: Atheneum Press, 1969.

Muse, Benjamin. *The American Negro Revolution.* Bloomington: Indiana University Press, 1968.

Neal, Lawrence P. "Black Power in the International Context." *The Black Power Revolt.* Edited by Floyd B. Barbour. Toronto: Collier-Macmillan Co., 1968.

Osofsky, Gilbert. *The Burden of Race.* Harper Torchbooks. New York: Harper and Row, 1967.

Quarles, Benjamin. *Frederick Douglass.* New York: Atheneum Press, 1969.

——. "Lord Dunmore as Liberator." *The Making of Black America.* Edited by August Meier and Elliott Rudwick. Vol. II. New York: Atheneum Press, 1969.

Terry, Wallace. "Black Soldiers and Vietnam." *The Black American: A Documentary History.* Edited by Leslie H. Fishel,

Jr., and Benjamin Quarles. New York: William Morrow and Co., 1970.

Wagstaff, Thomas. *Black Power: The Radical Response to White America.* Beverly Hills: Glencoe Press, 1969.

Washington, Booker T. *et al. The Negro Problem.* New York: Arno Press, 1969.

Wilkinson, Doris Y., ed. *Black Revolt: Strategies of Protest.* Berkeley: McCutchan Publishing Corp., 1969.

Williams, Jamye C., and Williams, McDonald, eds. *The Negro Speaks.* New York: Noble and Noble, Publishers, Inc., 1970.

X, Malcolm. *Malcolm X on Afro-American History.* New York: Pathfinder Press, 1970.

X, Malcolm, and Haley, Alex. *The Autobiography of Malcolm X.* New York: Grove Press, 1966.

Zinn, Howard. *Vietnam: The Logic of Withdrawal.* Boston: Beacon Press, 1967.


## *BIBLIOGRAPHY OF ARTICLES*

"Abolish the Draft! Enact the 'Freedom Budget!'" *Freedomways,* 6 (Fall, 1966), 293-295.

Barnett, Paul. "The Black Continentals." *Negro History Bulletin,* 33 (January 1970), 6-10.

"Black America 1970." *Time Magazine,* April 6, 1970, pp. 13-35, 45-100.

*Black Panther.* June 13, 1970.

Bonsal, Stephen. "The Negro Soldier in War and Peace." *North American Review* (186), June 1907.

Briggs, Cyril. "American Neo-Colonialism." *Liberator Magazine,* October 1966, pp. 14-17.

Browne, Robert S. "The Freedom Movement and the War in Vietnam." *Freedomways,* 5 (Fall, 1965), 467-480.

——. "Roots of U.S. Intervention in Cambodia." *Freedomways,* 10, No. 2 (Second Quarter, 1970), 115-123.

Butterfield, Roger. "The Mobilization of Black Strength." *Life Magazine,* December 6, 1968, pp. 93-106.

Carmichael, Stokely. "Black Power and the Third World." Printed in a pamphlet by the Southern Student Organizing Committee, Nashville, Tennessee, 1967, pp. 1-10.

——. "Power and Racism." Printed in a pamphlet by the Southern Student Organizing Committee, Nashville, Tennessee, 1966, pp. 1-9.

"Close Ranks." *Crisis Magazine,* July 1918, p. 111.

*Crisis Magazine,* July 1940.

Current, Gloster B. "The 61st Annual Convention: Arousing a National Storm." *Crisis Magazine,* August-September 1970, pp. 254-258, 271-274.

"Failure to Report for Induction." *Race Relations Law Reporter,* 12 (Winter, 1967), 19, 2311.

Fiske, John. "Crispus Attucks." *Negro History Bulletin,* 33 (March 1970), 58-68.

Franklin, John Hope, and Butterfield, Roger. "The Search for a Black Past." *Life Magazine,* November 22, 1968, pp. 90-120.

Friederich, Rudolf J. "54 Black Heroes: Medal of Honor Winners." *Crisis Magazine,* June-July 1969, pp. 243-245.

Harris, Janette H. "Crispus Attucks." *Negro History Bulletin,* 33 (March 1970), 69.

Hentoff, Nat. "Playboy Interview: Eldridge Cleaver." *Playboy Magazine,* December 1968, pp. 89-108, 238.

Jackson, Donald. "Unite or Perish." *Liberator Magazine,* February 1967, pp. 16-18.

——. "Black People and Vietnam." *Liberator Magazine,* December 1965, pp. 9-10.

Johnson, Thomas A. "Negroes in 'The Nam'." *Ebony Magazine,* August 1968, pp. 31-40.

King, Martin Luther. "A Time to Break Silence." *Freedomways,* 7 (Spring, 1967), 103-117.

——. "Speeches by the Reverend Doctor Martin Luther King, Jr., about the War in Vietnam," The Turnpike Press, Annandale, Virginia, pp. 1-25.

——. "Nonviolence and Racial Justice." *Christian Century,* LXXIV (February 6, 1957), pp. 165-167.

Lee, Bernard S. "We Must Continue to March." *Freedomways,* 6, No. 3 (Third Quarter, 1966), pp. 255-261.

Lester, Julius. "The Angry Children of Malcolm X." Printed in a pamphlet by the Southern Student Organizing Committee, Nashville, Tennessee, 1966, pp. 1-9.

"Letters to the Editor." *Ebony Magazine,* August 1968, pp. 14-16.

Lewis, David L. and Miao, Judy. "America's Greatest Negroes — A Survey." *Crisis Magazine,* January 1970, pp. 17-21.

Lewis, Flora. "The Rumble at Camp Lejeune." *Atlantic Magazine,* January 1970, pp. 35-41.

Llorens, David. "Why Negroes Re-enlist." *Ebony Magazine,* August 1968, pp. 87-92.

Mallette, Rev. Daniel J. "Vietnam; Only the Privileged are Exempt." *Liberator Magazine,* May 1966, pp. 16-17.

McLean, L. Deckle. "The Black Man and the Draft." *Ebony Magazine,* August 1968, pp. 61-66.

"Muhammad Ali — The Measure of a Man." *Freedomways,* 7 (Spring, 1967), 101-102.

*Muhammad Speaks.* April 25, 1969.

Minion, John A. "Negro Soldiers in the Confederate Army." *Crisis Magazine,* June-July 1970, pp. 230-232.

"Paradox of the Black Soldier." *Ebony Magazine,* August 1968, p. 142.

Parks, Gordon. "Eldridge Cleaver in Algiers, A Visit with Papa Rage." *Life Magazine,* February 6, 1970, pp. 20-25.

Patton, Gwendolyn. "Black People and War." *Liberator Magazine,* February 1967, pp. 10-11.

Pierce, Ponchitta, and Bailey, Peter. "The Returning Veteran." *Ebony Magazine,* August 1968, pp. 145-151.

"Report From Black America — A Newsweek Poll." *Newsweek Magazine,* June 30, 1969, pp. 16-35.

"Returning Soldiers." *Crisis Magazine,* May 1919, pp. 13-14.

Schanche, Don A. "Burn The Mother Down." *The Saturday Evening Post,* November 16, 1968, pp. 31-32, 65-71.

Snellings, Rolland. "Vietnam; Whitey: I Will Not Serve." *Liberator Magazine,* March 1966, pp. 8-9.

Storey, Robert. "Goodbye, Booker T." *Beacon Magazine* of Emerson College, Spring, 1970, pp. 17-20.

"The Boston Massacre and Crispus Attucks." *Negro History Bulletin,* 33 (March 1970), 56-57.

"The Two Presidents Johnson." *Freedomways,* 6 (Summer, 1966), 197-199.

"The War in Vietnam." *Freedomways,* 5 (Spring, 1965), pp. 229-230.

"The Terms Defined." *Ebony Magazine,* August 1970, p. 35.

"These Truly are the Brave." *Ebony Magazine,* August 1968, pp. 164-177.

U.S. Congress. Senate. Senator Morse requesting that testimony by A. Philip Randolph before the Armed Services Committee be printed in the Record. 80th Cong., 2d sess., April 12, 1948. *Congressional Record,* XCIV, 4312-4318.

Watts, Daniel H. "Reverend King and Vietnam." *Liberator Magazine,* May 1967, p. 3.

Wilson, C.E. "A Negro Looks at the War in Vietnam." *Liberator Magazine,* March 1966, pp. 31-32.

# BY AND ABOUT MALCOLM X

## FROM PATHFINDER

### *NEW!*
### *MALCOLM X TALKS TO YOUNG PEOPLE*

This new collection is made up of speeches and an interview given in Africa, Britain, and the United States, including several never before in print. $9.95.

## Malcolm X: The Last Speeches
First time in print.
$15.95

## Malcolm X Speaks
Cloth, now with index and photos.
$16.95

## By Any Means Necessary
by Malcolm X
$13.95

## Malcolm X on Afro-American History
New edition. $7.95

## Two Speeches by Malcolm X
$2.50

## The Last Year of Malcolm X
*The Evolution of a Revolutionary*
by George Breitman      $13.95

Order from Pathfinder. See front of book for addresses.